KELLEY CLEARY COFFEEN, PHD

TEX-MEX
DIABETES COOKING

MORE THAN 140 AUTHENTIC SOUTHWESTERN FAVORITES

American
Diabetes
Association®

Associate Publisher, Books, Abe Ogden; *Director, Book Operations,* Victor Van Beuren; *Managing Editor, Books,* John Clark; *Associate Director, Book Marketing,* Annette Reape; *Acquisitions Editor,* Jaclyn Konich; *Senior Manager, Book Editing,* Lauren Wilson; *Project Manager,* Amnet Systems; *Composition,* Amnet Systems; *Cover Design,* Vis-à-vis Creative; *Photographer,* Mittera; *Printer,* Bang Printing.

Printed in the United States of America

1 3 5 7 9 10 8 6 4 2

The suggestions and information contained in this publication are generally consistent with the *Standards of Medical Care in Diabetes* and other policies of the American Diabetes Association, but they do not represent the policy or position of the Association or any of its boards or committees. Reasonable steps have been taken to ensure the accuracy of the information presented. However, the American Diabetes Association cannot ensure the safety or efficacy of any product or service described in this publication. Individuals are advised to consult a physician or other appropriate health care professional before undertaking any diet or exercise program or taking any medication referred to in this publication. Professionals must use and apply their own professional judgment, experience, and training and should not rely solely on the information contained in this publication before prescribing any diet, exercise, or medication. The American Diabetes Association—its officers, directors, employees, volunteers, and members—assumes no responsibility or liability for personal or other injury, loss, or damage that may result from the suggestions or information in this publication.

Madelyn Wheeler conducted the internal review of this book to ensure that it meets American Diabetes Association guidelines.

∞ The paper in this publication meets the requirements of the ANSI Standard Z39.48-1992 (permanence of paper).

ADA titles may be purchased for business or promotional use or for special sales. To purchase more than 50 copies of this book at a discount, or for custom editions of this book with your logo, contact the American Diabetes Association at the address below or at booksales@diabetes.org.

American Diabetes Association
2451 Crystal Drive, Suite 900
Arlington, VA 22202

DOI: 10.2337/9781580406659

Library of Congress Cataloging-in-Publication Data
Names: Coffeen, Kelley, author.
Title: Tex-Mex diabetes cooking : more than 140 authentic Southwestern
    favorites / Kelley Cleary Coffeen.
Description: Arlington : American Diabetes Association, [2018]
Identifiers: LCCN 2017013401 | ISBN 9781580406659
Subjects: LCSH: Diabetes—Diet therapy—Recipes. | Mexican American cooking.
Classification: LCC RC662 .C588 2018 | DDC 641.5/6314—dc23
LC record available at https://lccn.loc.gov/2017013401

I dedicate this book to my mother, Frances Janet Cleary,
a beautiful lady who inspired this collection of recipes by
her love for rellenos, tacos, and enchiladas, and
her daily struggle with diabetes.
Her love and laughter are always with me.

Table of Contents

Acknowledgments ix

Introduction xi

Lifestyle Trends for Diabetes xiii
Water—Benefits for People with Diabetes xiii
Get Moving: The Health Benefits of Walking xiii

Tex-Mex Flavor Essentials xv
Fresh Chiles xv
Herbs xvi
Spices xvi
Greens and Nonstarchy Vegetables xvii
Whole Grains and Starchy Vegetables xviii
Other Vegetables and Fruits xviii
Cheeses and Other Dairy xix
Legumes and Nuts xx
Healthy Fats xx
Fish High in Omega-3 Fatty Acids xxi
Alcohol xxi
Tips for Tex-Mex Cooking for People with Diabetes xxi
Kitchen Techniques, Tools, and Equipment xxii

Cocktails and More 1
Agua Frescas 2
Margarita Martini 3
Fresh Tequila Sunrise 4
Fresh Mexican Mimosa 6
Margarita Rounds 7
Sparkling Margarita Punch 8
Frozen Margarita 9
Spicy Margarita 10
Fresco White Sangria 11
Fruity Red Sangria 12
Michelada 13
Tequila Shots and Sangrita Chaser 14

Paloma Fresco 15
Mexican Café 16
Mexican Hot Chocolate 17

Bites and Starters 19
Baked Crispy Corn Tortilla Chips 20
Pita Chips 21
Ceviche 22
Mini Shrimp Shooters 23
Savory Mini Tostadas 24
Mini Hummus Tostaditos 25
Tex-Mex Nachos 26
Saucy Loaded Nachos 27
Tres Quesos Street Nachos 28
Classic Guacamole 29
Fresh Green Chile Guacamole 30
Charred Corn and Avocado Toss 31
Black Bean Layered Spread 32
Chile Bruschetta 33
Chile con Queso 35
Spinach and Artichoke Queso 36
Mini Chimis 37
Chile Pinwheels 38
Jalapeño Pinwheels 39
Roasted Green Chile Cheese Crisp 41
Quesadillas de Fresco 42
Pineapple and Chile Quesadillas 43
Chicken and Sweet Potato Quesadillas 44

Salsas and More 47
Pico de Gallo 48
Tex-Mex Salsa 49
Roasted Tomatillo Chile Sauce 50
Citrusy Salsa 51
Spicy Corn Salsa 52

Mexican White Sauce	53
Classic Queso Sauce	54
Pickled Onions	55
Roasted Pineapple Salsa	57
Coleslaw Relish	58
Jicama Salsa	59
Chile Cream Sauce	60
Tex-Mex Chile Gravy	61
Fresh Veggie Enchilada Sauce	62
Red Enchilada Sauce	63
Green Chile Enchilada Sauce	64
Sweet Chile Sauce	65
Sidebar:	
Red Chile Purée	66

Tortillas and Breads 69

Fresh Whole-Grain Flour Tortillas (8-inch)	70
Fresh Whole-Grain Flour Tortillas (10-inch)	71
Fresh Corn Tortillas	72
Light Sopapillas	73
Sidebars:	
Baked Tostada Shells	74
Reheating Tortillas	75

Breakfast Favorites 77

Breakfast Quesadilla	79
Tex-Mex Breakfast Tacos	80
Huevos Rancheros	81
Chorizo, Potato, and Egg Burrito—Smothered	82
Chilaquiles with Eggs	83
Chile Papas	84
Pan Huevos with Avocado	85
Spiced Fresh Fruit and Yogurt Parfait	86
Whole-Wheat Morning Toast with Cajeta and Coconut	87
Mexican Bread Pudding with Fresh Berries	89

Soups and Stews 91

Green Chile Corn Chowder	93
Albondigas	95
Red Chile Posole	96
Chicken Tortilla Soup	97
Green Chile Stew	98
Tex-Mex Chile con Carne	99

Tostadas, Tacos, Tamales, Burritos, Enchiladas, and More 101

Tostadas	103
Frijoles Tostadas	103
Roasted Sweet Potato Tostadas	104
Ceviche Tostadas	105
Chile con Carne Tostadas	107
Tacos	108
Fajita Tacos	108
Classic Crispy Tacos	109
Classic Rolled Tacos	110
Grilled Carne Asada Tacos	111
Seared Sirloin Tacos with Guacamole	112
Tacos al Pastor	113
Pork Carnitas Tacos	114
Chipotle BBQ Pork Soft Tacos	115
Speedy Roasted Chicken Soft Tacos	116
Chicken Tacos Verde	117
Grilled Mesquite Chicken Tacos	118
Quick Turkey Club Tacos	119
Poblano and Potato Tacos with Chile Cream Sauce	120
Spicy Black Bean Tacos	121
Avocado Corn Soft Tacos	122
Crispy Zucchini Tacos	123
Tex-Mex Shrimp Tacos	125
South Texas Fish Tacos	126
Grilled Halibut Tacos	127
No-Beef Taquitos	128
Veggie Taquitos	129
Sweet Potato Taquitos	130
Baked Chicken Flautas	131
Bean and Rice Flautas	132

Tamales 133
 Smoked Cheddar Cheese and Green
  Chile Tamales 133
   Sidebar:
    Tamale Preparation 134
 Spinach Asparagus Tamales 135
 Red Chile Tamales 137
Burritos 138
 Fiber-Full Burrito Bowls 138
 Machaca Burritos 139
 Chile Verde Burritos 141
 Bean and Cheese Chimichangas 142
Enchiladas 143
 Cheesy Green Chile Enchiladas 143
 Tex-Mex Cheese Enchiladas 145
 Sour Cream Green Chile Enchiladas 146
 Red Chile Beefy Street Enchiladas 147
 Stacked Saucy Enchiladas with Fresh Greens 148
And More 149
 Torta de Fresco (Mexican Sandwich) 149
 Baked Chile Rellenos 150
 Savory Stuffed Sopapillas 151
  Sidebars:
   Roasted Green Chiles 152
   Shredded Beef 153
   Red Chile Pork 154
   Shredded Chicken 155
   Tex-Mex Shrimp 156

Savory Sides 159
 Mexican Rice 160
 Green Chile Rice 161
 Zucchini and Corn Medley
  (Calabacitas) 162
 Tangy Mexican Slaw 163
 Pinto Beans 164
 Refried Beans 165
 Fresh-Mex Greens with Chipotle
  Honey Sauce 166
 Papas and Queso 167
 Chopped Mexican Salad with Lime 169

Little Sweets 171
 Baked Sopapilla Bites 172
 Quick Churros with Coconut Sauce 173
 Mini Flan Cheesecakes 174
 Sweet Tortilla Triangles 175
 Tres Leches Parfait 177
 Mini Apple Chimichangas 179
 Colada Parfait 180
 Crispy Ice Cream Scoops with Cajeta
  Sauce 181
 Wine Margarita Sorbet 182
 Mi Chocolate Cake 183
 Saucy Pralines 184

Index 187

Acknowledgments

Such a great experience! I am honored to work with the American Diabetes Association on this cookbook. Knowledge is power, so highlighting the wonderful flavors of Tex-Mex and Mexican cuisine while staying within the American Diabetes Association guidelines is a game changer for so many.

I want to thank Lisa and Sally Ekus, my literary agents, at The Lisa Ekus Group. Lisa and Sally, your patience, support, and keen sense of what your authors can do is appreciated. Thank you for sharing your literary skills, insight, and connections during this project. I appreciate the challenging work we do together. Victor Van Beuren, I am forever thankful to you for believing in me. A huge thank-you to my editor, Lauren Wilson, who patiently led me through the photography and editing process; you are amazing. And thank you to Jennifer Crane, the editorial project manager, for your hard work and attention to detail. Finally, thank you Janice Shay for your guidance early on.

Sadly, I lost my mom during the writing of this book. Her journey with diabetes was not unique, but exemplifies the challenges that come with this disease. I want to thank the American Diabetes Association and all those in the medical field focused on diabetes education and wellness. I appreciate you!

Thank you to my family for all the fun tastings, foodie chats, hugs of encouragement, and laughs. I appreciate you all! A final and big "gracias!" to my culinary crew for your culinary expertise and inspiration. Near and far, you are always impacting what I do in the kitchen. Time for margaritas!

Finally, I must acknowledge God's grace in my life.

Introduction

I often say that Mexican cuisine is the world's comfort food with a little kick, and Tex-Mex is no different. It's comforting because it is full of hearty ingredients like roasted meats, lentils and beans, fresh veggies, seafood, fish, and rich cheeses. The kick comes from natural herbs, earthy spices, and the flavorful sauces and salsas that crown each dish. Tex-Mex has the added incentives of being inexpensive, quick to prepare, easy to serve, and packed with layers of flavor in every bite. Hand-held favorites like tacos and burritos, and other dishes—like tostadas and nachos—that are easy to eat without utensils, continue to be universal culinary sensations, encouraging a relaxed camaraderie among guests, young and old alike.

Tex-Mex Diabetes Cooking is full of amazingly delicious ways to reduce carbs and eat healthy, with tips and ingredient ideas to lighten each recipe.

Whether you are planning a fiesta—complete with tasty margaritas, a backdrop of piñatas, and a mariachi band—or simply preparing a nutritious weekday meal for your family, *Tex-Mex Diabetes Cooking* will give you a healthy taste of some south-of-the border fun! You can turn a typical Tuesday night into Taco Tuesday, enticing everyone to come to the table. All of a sudden it's a party—just beware, the neighbors might drop by as well! That is why I love Mexican fare: It is so delicious—and FUN! Specifically, Tex-Mex cuisine is even more amazing. Rooted in the state of Texas's Tejano culture with traces of Native American, Mexican, and Spanish cultures intertwined, it is a culinary adventure all on its own. Over the years, Tex-Mex has evolved into a style of ethnic cuisine that features yellow cheeses melted over enchiladas; gravies and sauces laced with rich combinations of cumin, oregano, and garlic; creative and tasty ways to use corn tortillas; and the evolution of the tortilla chip. Its bicultural roots of Mexico and North America have brought us a Mexican-American fare that has blended flavors and cooking techniques and has stood the test of time.

In *Tex-Mex Diabetes Cooking*, I embrace this historically meat-laden, cheesy, spicy cuisine and add vegetables, herbs, and reduced-fat ingredients along with alternative cooking techniques to embrace the cuisine, elevating it to a level of healthy goodness. Classics such as chile con queso, chile con carne, cheese enchiladas, chile gravy, nachos, refried beans, fajitas, breakfast tacos, sorbet, and pralines have been reworked to give the most flavor with the least amount of carbohydrates and fat.

I offer a variety of techniques and ingredients that help cut the calorie count, fat content, and carbohydrates while increasing protein levels in a manner that is sensitive to people with diabetes. By making every carbohydrate count and by incorporating the superfoods that I love to cook with, I have brought together a healthy array of Southwest favorites without losing the traditional Mexican flavors.

Knowledge is power for healthy eating. Offering low-carb recipes that are especially healthful for people with diabetes—and including the nutritional information with each recipe—is critical to preparing food that helps you manage diabetes successfully. With type 2 diabetes at an all-time high among Americans, this book is key to solving the dilemma that home cooks face in preparing great-tasting Tex-Mex cuisine that is also low-carb and friendly to people with diabetes.

In *Tex-Mex Diabetes Cooking*, I have infused fresh produce and herbs, along with natural proteins, with unique cooking techniques to reduce the calories and cholesterol-inducing fats.

I hope you enjoy these lighter Tex-Mex favorites, enhanced with good nutrients.

Kelley Cleary Coffeen

Lifestyle Trends for Diabetes

Water—Benefits for People with Diabetes

You'd think it would be easy, drinking water. But I really have to focus on getting my daily intake, and I don't always do it. It is hard to drink water, especially in the winter months. But the benefits make it important enough to talk about, especially for people with diabetes:

- Dehydration can cause your blood glucose levels to rise.
- Water helps keep you hydrated and feeling full.
- When you're thirsty, your body is telling you that you're dehydrated. There are other signs that point to dehydration—for example, cramping and headaches.

Tip

I have found that drinking a large glass of water before every meal curbs my appetite. Also, before a meal is a key point in time to get at least some water intake done. Mealtime is an easy point in the day to remind yourself to drink water! But even this little trick takes practice. Put a reminder in your phone or a note in your lunchbox or near the stove or the dining table.

Make It Interesting . . .

- Adding fruits to water can enhance your experience in drinking water. Go all in—use a water bottle with an infuser, adding slices of orange, lemon, or lime. Combine a few favorite herbs and fruit flavors in a pitcher, and chill for a couple of hours; strawberries and lemon, peaches and raspberries, even cucumbers and rosemary are delicious combinations.
- Make a game out of it and compare notes with a friend—the buddy system works and keeps us accountable!
- Don't forget that nonstarchy vegetables are also full of water. So fill half your plate with natural goodness.

Get Moving: The Health Benefits of Walking

Studies show that walking (and other forms of regular physical activity) can improve your health over your life span. Walking can help to:

- Improve your blood pressure, help lower your cholesterol, lower your stress levels, and help you deal with depression;

- Reduce risks for such chronic diseases as heart disease and dementia; and
- In many cases, lower blood glucose levels.

I think walking is one of the easiest ways to start improving your personal health. I like to use my walks as "me" time. I download podcasts on fashion, entertainment, current events, and financial news. This is a time I can have all to myself. There have been days when I started out on a 30-minute walk and came back an hour later. Just 30 minutes a day can add years to your life. You deserve that!

Tips

- Form a walking group: Call your friends or post it on social media.
- Treat your walk as time for yourself. Enhance it with audio entertainment—such as recordings of your favorite music or podcasts you've been waiting to listen to.
- Join a local walking club.
- Create a schedule that includes 20 to 30 minutes a day during the week, and a special-location walk on Saturday.
- Invest in good walking shoes, clothes, and protective gear. Be safe!

Tex-Mex Flavor Essentials

Many foods recommended by the American Diabetes Association are a natural partner to Tex-Mex cuisine. Beans, green leafy vegetables, citrus, sweet potatoes, berries, tomatoes, fish, whole grains, nuts, and fat-free dairy and healthy fats are integral to my healthy Tex-Mex recipes. All of these foods can be part of a diabetes-friendly diet and provide key nutrients, such as calcium, potassium, fiber, magnesium, and vitamins A, C, and E.

Fresh Chiles

Chipotle Chile in Adobo Sauce

A sauce made of dried jalapeño peppers marinated in a smoky blend of onions, tomatoes, and garlic. Most often, this sauce is canned and is available in the Mexican food section at local grocery stores.

Dried Red Chile Pods

Ready to be rehydrated, blended, and used in sauces. Available in plastic bags in the produce section or Mexican food section at local grocery stores.

Jalapeño

A small, bright green chile, ranging from mild to hot. Typically used in salsas, sauces, and as garnish for many Mexican dishes. Available fresh in the produce section at local grocery stores.

Pickled Jalapeños

Small green chiles marinated in herbs, oil, and vinegar. Available canned or bottled in the Mexican food section or condiment section at most local grocery stores.

Anaheim/New Mexico Chile

A long, thin green chile with medium to hot varieties, used in salsas and sauces and in many Mexican dishes. Usually roasted, seeded, and peeled (page 152) for best flavor. Available fresh in the produce section of most local grocery stores. Roasted green chiles can also be found in the frozen-food section at most local grocery stores or online.

Poblano Chile

A larger, dark green chile used in salsas and sauces. Has a rich, earthy flavor and is mild to medium in heat. Tastes best when roasted, seeded, and peeled (page 152). Available fresh in the produce section of local grocery stores.

Serrano Chile

A small, thin green chile, smaller and usually hotter than a jalapeño. Available fresh in the produce section of local grocery stores.

Yellow Chile

A small yellow chile, with a waxy appearance, mild in flavor. Available fresh in the produce section of local grocery stores.

Herbs

Cilantro

A leafy green herb with a distinctive, pungent flavor. It is used widely in Mexican cuisine, especially as a garnish and in salsas.

Sage

A leafy green herb with a soft, sweet/savory flavor.

Rosemary

An aromatic herb that has a citrusy pine flavor.

Flat-Leaf Parsley (also called Italian parsley)

This mild herb adds color and texture to marinades and sauces.

Spices

Cayenne Pepper

This is a chili powder that has a hot, edgy flavor. It spices up sauces, stews, and salsas.

Chili Powder

Red powder derived from dried ground chile pods.

Cinnamon

This fragrant spice blends well with fruits and chocolate. It has a spicy clove flavor.

Cumin

This spice has a distinctive earthy, nutty flavor and aroma. Just a pinch adds flavor to sauces, gravies, and marinades.

Chipotle Chile Powder

Dried ground chipotle chiles, blended with oregano, garlic, and cumin.

Crushed Red Pepper Flakes

These dried red pepper flakes add heat to salsas, marinades, and sauces.

Mexican Oregano

Stronger in flavor and with a larger blossom than regular oregano; has a full, robust flavor.

Vanilla

A liquid flavoring that adds a hint of sweetness and balance.

Greens and Nonstarchy Vegetables

Fresh vegetables and greens expand the flavor and volume of Tex-Mex cuisine, adding extra freshness and texture to every dish. A single serving of my Red Chile Beefy Street Enchiladas (page 147) topped with a handful of salad mix creates layers of flavor and texture while adding some extra nutrients. Light queso wrapped around spinach and artichoke hearts builds volume and offers a healthy, satisfying appetizer. I like to investigate the varieties of salad mix and greens in my local market's produce department. Fresh shredded or chopped greens combined with a pinch of fresh herbs add volume and flavor and create healthy new favorites.

Taking time to buy good-quality produce at the last moment will give you the best results. I shop the local farmer's market, micro farms, and local grocers for variety and freshness. Spinach, collards, kale—these powerhouse foods are low in calories and carbohydrate. I use them to increase volume and garnish my Tex-Mex dishes.

Nonstarchy Vegetables

Typically, nonstarchy vegetables have about 5 grams of carbohydrate in 1/2 cup cooked or 1 cup raw. Most of the carbohydrate is fiber, so I like to add these tasty fresh vegetables to tacos, stews, soups, and appetizers. Chopped or shredded, they make the perfect garnish.

Nonstarchy vegetables include: artichoke hearts; asparagus; baby corn; bean sprouts; cabbage (green, bok choy, Chinese); coleslaw (packaged, no dressing); cucumber; greens (collard, kale, mustard, turnip); jicama; onions; peppers; radishes; salad greens (chicory, endive, escarole, lettuce, romaine, spinach, arugula, radicchio, watercress); sprouts; and squash.

Whole Grains and Starchy Vegetables

I select grains that are the most nutritious: whole grains. Whole grains are rich in vitamins, minerals, phytochemicals, and fiber.

Whole Grains

It's the germ and bran of the whole grain you're after; together they contain all the nutrients a grain product has to offer. A few more of the nutrients that these foods offer are magnesium, chromium, omega-3 fatty acids, and folate. So whole-grain tortillas are a wonderful choice for Tex-Mex recipes.

Whole grains are sometimes hard to find. The best way to ensure that a product is made with whole grains is to look for the following as the first ingredient listed:

- Bulgur (cracked wheat)
- Whole-wheat flour
- Whole oats/oatmeal
- Whole-grain corn/cornmeal
- Brown rice
- Wild rice
- Buckwheat
- Buckwheat flour
- Quinoa

Starchy Vegetables

Starchy vegetables are good sources of vitamins, minerals, and fiber. Starchy vegetables have more calories and carbohydrates than nonstarchy vegetables, but they can still be part of a healthy meal. Sweet potatoes are an example of a starchy vegetable packed full of vitamin A and fiber. Try them in place of regular potatoes for a nutrient-rich alternative.

Other Vegetables and Fruits

Corn

This vegetable adds fiber to the diet and is a good source of vitamin B. It has a hint of sweetness.

Potato

This versatile root vegetable can add volume as well as enhance the flavor of a dish.

Butternut Squash

This squash has a sweet, nutty taste.

Citrus Fruit

Grapefruit, oranges, lemons, limes—these citrusy gems will provide your daily dose of soluble fiber and vitamin C. Whether you're adding a spritz of lime over grilled sirloin or creating a citrus salsa, there are so many ways to add citrus to Tex-Mex cuisine.

Berries

Blueberries, strawberries, and raspberries are all packed with antioxidants, vitamins, and fiber. I use berries in salsas and sauces as well as in desserts.

Tomatoes

No matter how you like your tomatoes—puréed, raw, or in a sauce—you're eating vital nutrients like vitamin C, iron, and vitamin E. Using tomatoes as garnish or as the basis for salsas and sauces makes it a key ingredient in Tex-Mex cooking.

Cheeses and Other Dairy

Cheeses

Cheese is a pillar ingredient of Tex-Mex cooking. Besides my queso recipes, I like to add cheese as an accent to the layers of flavor in many of my Tex-Mex dishes. So selecting lower-fat dairy products in general and finding flavorful cheeses that are healthy and lower-fat have been a priority for this book. While reduced-fat cheddar cheese and Monterey Jack cheese are always popular, many new healthy cheese blends are readily available as well. Explore, taste, and find your favorite.

Mexican Cheeses

I love the cheeses of Mexico, such as asadero, cotija, and queso fresco. These melting cheeses or hard/semifirm cheeses are readily available in most local grocery stores. I like to melt a creamy soft cheese like asadero over enchiladas. Fresh Mexican cheeses such as queso fresco and cotija can be crumbled and sprinkled on top of so many Tex-Mex dishes as garnishes.

Reduced-Fat Milk and Yogurt

In addition to building strong bones and providing calcium for strong teeth, many fortified dairy products are a good source of vitamin D. More research is emerging on the connection between vitamin D and good health. Dairy products with lower levels of fat make good choices for quesos and sauces.

To keep my Tex-Mex recipes low in carbs and fat, I try to incorporate fat-free or low-fat (1%) milk, yogurt, and sour cream wherever possible. Paying attention to taste and texture, I have found some tasteful combinations. Plain fat-free yogurt (regular or Greek yogurt); fat-free light yogurt (regular or Greek yogurt); unflavored fortified soy milk; or soy milk, rice milk, or almond milk are all worthy of consideration for sauces, quesos, and garnish.

Legumes and Nuts

Legumes

Legumes and beans are very high in fiber, giving you about one-third of your daily requirement in just half a cup, and are also good sources of magnesium and potassium. They are considered starchy vegetables, but half a cup provides as much protein as an ounce of meat without the saturated fat. To save time, you can use canned beans, but be sure to drain and rinse them to get rid of as much sodium as possible.

Black Beans
These black, kidney-shaped beans—available dried or canned—have an earthy flavor. Dried black beans can be cooked like Pinto Beans (page 164). Canned beans should be rinsed before using.

Pinto Beans
Pinto beans are a fat-free, high-protein legume that adds fiber to any recipe. Cooked Pinto Beans (page 164) can be mashed and reheated, creating Refried Beans (page 165) for use as a filling and as a side dish. Canned pinto beans are a convenient choice, and they have good flavor and texture; look for a low-sodium version, and rinse them before using.

Red Beans
Red or "kidney" beans have a good texture and are rich in flavor when cooked. Canned kidney beans have a soft texture. Rinse them before using.

Nuts

An ounce of nuts can go a long way in providing key healthy fats and managing hunger. Other benefits are a dose of magnesium and fiber. Some nuts and seeds, such as walnuts and flax seeds, also contain omega-3 fatty acids.

Healthy Fats

Focusing on healthy fats like avocado, pecans, cashews, almonds, canola and olive oil, and sesame seeds is easy when you're making my Tex-Mex recipes. Healthy fats are thoroughly integrated into the recipes in this book. These monounsaturated fats—known as "good" or "healthy" fats—can help lower bad (LDL) cholesterol.

Fish High in Omega-3 Fatty Acids

Salmon, albacore tuna, halibut, and cod are high in omega-3 fatty acids. Fish tacos and grilled fish with fresh salsa or enchilada sauce are tasty Tex-Mex dishes with a big helping of omega-3 fatty acids.

Alcohol

According to the American Diabetes Association, alcohol is *not* off limits to people with diabetes or those watching their blood glucose levels. However, moderation is key. Women should have no more than one drink per day. Men should have no more than two drinks per day. One drink is equal to a 12-ounce beer, a 5-ounce glass of wine, or 1 1/2 ounces distilled spirits (tequila, vodka, whiskey, gin, etc.).

Tips for Tex-Mex Cooking for People with Diabetes

- Try a variety of reduced-fat cheddar and white cheeses and find a few notable favorites. They're typically found in the specialty cheese section or deli section of your local grocery store.
- Use reduced-fat milks, milk substitutes, fat-free yogurts, and sour creams for quesos, side dishes, casseroles, fillings, and sauces.
- Grill, bake, roast, and lightly sauté lean trimmed meats and poultry for fillings in tacos, tamales, and burritos.
- Bake or skillet-warm tortillas instead of frying them. For a crispy finish on tacos and chips, spray the tortillas with cooking spray and bake them in an oven preheated to 400°F or 425°F.
- Increase the volume of a taco or tostada by topping it with a variety of fresh vegetables: try leafy green lettuce, baby spinach, thinly sliced sweet or red onions, diced yellow squash, chopped zucchini, or diced cherry tomatoes.
- Use low-sodium beef broth and chicken broth to flavor soups, stews, and sauces.
- Blend chile spices with fat-free sour cream.
- Fresh seasonings begin with fresh herbs. Add fresh minced herbs such as chives and cilantro to sauces or fat-free plain yogurt for a unique and healthy garnish.
- Infuse foods with the distinctive flavors of onion, lemon, and lime.
- Smart cocktails can be created with sugar-free syrups and low-sugar juices and mixers. Make thoughtful choices in your selection of spirits, mixers, and garnish.
- Watching calories and carbohydrates is easy if you plan and prepare ahead of time. Be adventurous: mix and match flavors—citrus with chile, sweet with savory. Add spices to meats and poultry and to sauces and salsas. Find your favorite combinations.

Kitchen Techniques, Tools, and Equipment

- Tortilla press
- Tortilla warmer
- Skillet
- Digital instant-read thermometer
- Tongs
- Cutting boards
- Cheese grater
- Dry measuring cups
- Liquid measuring cups
- Whisks
- Mixing bowls
- Small serving bowls
- Small chafing dish
- Hand-held citrus juicer
- Zester

Cocktails and More

Tex-Mex gatherings are always a celebration. Whether it is a small get-together or just dinner out on the patio, a good cocktail or alcoholic beverage adds fun to any meal.. Cut calories and reduce sugar levels by using fresh fruit and sugar-free syrups and selecting the best spirits, mixers, and garnish. Watching calories and carbohydrates is easy if you plan and prepare ahead of time. Adding sugar-free mixers such as sparkling water, seltzer, and tonic gives the healthy options you need.

This collection will help you create tantalizing drinks, composed of subtle spirits and unique flavors for memorable cocktails with a moderate amount of alcohol. Celebrate and enjoy margaritas, mimosas, micheladas, and other Mexican cocktails.

Agua Frescas 2

Margarita Martini 3

Fresh Tequila Sunrise 4

Fresh Mexican Mimosa 6

Margarita Rounds 7

Sparkling Margarita Punch 8

Frozen Margarita. 9

Spicy Margarita 10

Fresco White Sangria 11

Fruity Red Sangria 12

Michelada 13

Tequila Shots and Sangrita Chaser. 14

Paloma Fresco. 15

Mexican Café 16

Mexican Hot Chocolate. 17

Agua Frescas

Serves: 10
Serving Size: 1 cup
Prep Time: 20 minutes
Chill Time: 1 hour

Choices/Exchanges

Free food

Basic Nutritional Values

Calories	15
Calories from Fat	0
Total Fat	0.0 g
Saturated Fat	0.0 g
Trans Fat	0.0 g
Cholesterol	0 mg
Sodium	0 mg
Potassium	80 mg
Total Carbohydrate	4 g
Dietary Fiber	1 g
Sugars	2 g
Protein	0 g
Phosphorus	10 mg

Flavored water continues to be a trend north of the border, but it is nothing new in the Mexican culture. Large glass containers of agua fresca line the taco stands at the open markets throughout Mexico. Enjoy this light, refreshing fruited water infused with peaches, kiwi, mangoes, or berries. I make a batch every few days, especially in the warmer months—it can be a powerful tool in curbing your appetite.

4 cups fresh strawberries, hulled and sliced
6 cups cold water
Juice of 3 limes
2 Tbsp sugar-free strawberry syrup
6 whole fresh strawberries
Ice

1. In a blender, combine half of the strawberries and half of the water. Strain strawberry mixture through a sieve into a pitcher or glass jar. Discard solids. Repeat with remaining strawberries and water.
2. Stir in lime juice and strawberry syrup. Place in the refrigerator and chill for at least 1 hour or up to 3 hours. Serve over ice. Garnish with whole strawberry.

Note: Instead of strawberries, substitute 4 cups of any of the following: raspberries, blueberries, mango chunks (seeded and peeled), papaya. Follow Steps 1–2. For a sweeter beverage, add honey to taste.

Margarita Martini

This simple margarita is a reflection of the traditional cocktail served with Tex-Mex cuisine. Light flavors of citrus blend well with the tequila for a robust libation.

Cracked ice
1 oz silver tequila
1 oz sugar-free lemon-flavored syrup (such as Torani)
1 oz fresh-squeezed lime juice
1 fresh lime peel twist

1. Fill a shaker half full with cracked ice.
2. Pour in tequila, syrup, and lime juice.
3. Shake well and strain into a chilled martini glass.
4. Garnish with lime twist.

Serves: 1
Serving Size: 3 oz
Prep Time: 12 minutes
Cook Time: N/A

Choices/Exchanges

1 Alcohol

Basic Nutritional Values

Calories	80
Calories from Fat	0
Total Fat	0.0 g
Saturated Fat	0.0 g
Trans Fat	0.0 g
Cholesterol	0 mg
Sodium	10 mg
Potassium	25 mg
Total Carbohydrate	2 g
Dietary Fiber	0 g
Sugars	0 g
Protein	0 g
Phosphorus	5 mg

Fresh Tequila Sunrise

Serves: 1
Serving Size: 6 1/2 oz
Prep Time: 12 minutes
Cook Time: N/A

Choices/Exchanges

1 Fruit, 1 Alcohol

Basic Nutritional Values

Calories	140
Calories from Fat	0
Total Fat	0.0 g
Saturated Fat	0.0 g
Trans Fat	0.0 g
Cholesterol	0 mg
Sodium	5 mg
Potassium	270 mg
Total Carbohydrate	15 g
Dietary Fiber	2 g
Sugars	11 g
Protein	1 g
Phosphorus	25 mg

Fresh flavors of citrus make this delightful cocktail perfect any time of year. Served unshaken or stirred, it gets its name from the layers of color. A Tequila Sunrise is typically served with grenadine, which is high in sugar. To reduce those sugar levels, use a sugar-free fruit syrup or sugar-free jam instead. Sparkling water increases the volume of the drink and reduces the calories.

Cracked ice
1 oz silver tequila
4 oz fresh-squeezed or reduced-sugar orange juice
1 oz sparkling water
1/2 oz sugar-free raspberry jam (see Note)
1 lime wedge

1. Fill a highball-style glass with cracked ice.
2. In a separate glass, combine the tequila, orange juice, and sparkling water. Pour this mixture over the ice in the highball glass.
3. Tip the highball glass and slowly pour the raspberry jam down the side. The jam will go straight to the bottom and rise up slowly through the drink. Garnish with lime wedge.

Note: To use the sugar-free raspberry jam (a store-bought brand of your choice) as needed for this recipe, warm it until it liquefies, then cool it to room temperature.

Spicy Margarita, p. 10; Fresh Mexican Mimosa, p. 6; Fresh Tequila Sunrise, p. 4

Fresh Mexican Mimosa

Serves: 1
Serving Size: 4 1/2 oz
Prep Time: 10 minutes
Cook Time: N/A

Choices/Exchanges

1/2 Fruit, 1 Alcohol

Basic Nutritional Values

Calories	120
Calories from Fat	0
Total Fat	0.0 g
Saturated Fat	0.0 g
Trans Fat	0.0 g
Cholesterol	0 mg
Sodium	0 mg
Potassium	170 mg
Total Carbohydrate	8 g
Dietary Fiber	0 g
Sugars	6 g
Protein	1 g
Phosphorus	25 mg

There is something festive about this citrusy drink. It is the perfect daytime cocktail. The tequila adds a little kick.

1/2 oz tequila
2 oz fresh-squeezed or reduced-sugar orange juice
2 oz dry champagne or dry white wine (see Note)
2 fresh raspberries

1. Pour tequila and orange juice into a champagne flute.
2. Top with champagne and berries.

Note: Reduce the calories in this drink by replacing the champagne or wine with sparkling water.

Margarita Rounds

Gelatin shots are a slurpy, fun way to get a party going! These sugar-free gelatin shots are great take-alongs for an outdoor happy hour or beach party.

1 (0.3-oz) package sugar-free lime gelatin
1 cup boiling water
1/2 cup cold water
1/2 cup tequila

1. Empty gelatin powder into a large mixing bowl and add boiling water. Stir until the gelatin is completely dissolved, about 2–3 minutes.
2. Slowly add the cold water and tequila. Mix well.
3. Pour into 2-oz plastic cups, one-half to three-quarters full. Chill until firm. (Attach lids if transporting.)

Serves: 10
Serving Size: 3 Tbsp
Prep Time: 8 minutes
Chill Time: 2 to 3 hours

Choices/Exchanges
1/2 Alcohol

Basic Nutritional Values

Calories 30
  Calories from Fat 0
Total Fat . . . . .0.0 g
  Saturated Fat . . . . .0.0 g
  Trans Fat . . . . .0.0 g
Cholesterol . . . . 0 mg
Sodium . . . . 20 mg
Potassium . . . . 0 mg
Total Carbohydrate. . . . . 0 g
  Dietary Fiber . . . . 0 g
  Sugars . . . . 0 g
Protein . . . . 0 g
Phosphorus . . . . .15 mg

Sparkling Margarita Punch

Serves: 8
Serving Size: About 6 oz
Prep Time: 12 minutes
Cook Time: N/A

Choices/Exchanges

1/2 Alcohol

Basic Nutritional Values

Calories................... 40
  Calories from Fat 0
Total Fat .... 0.0 g
  Saturated Fat .... 0.0 g
  Trans Fat .... 0.0 g
Cholesterol .... 0 mg
Sodium .... 20 mg
Potassium .... 10 mg
Total Carbohydrate........ 1 g
  Dietary Fiber .... 0 g
  Sugars................... 0 g
Protein .... 0 g
Phosphorus .... 0 mg

This refreshing margarita punch is quick to make and is a real crowd-pleaser. It will become a citrusy bubbly favorite. Sparkling water lightens it up.

5 oz sugar-free lime-flavored syrup (such as Torani)
4 oz silver tequila
2 (16.9-oz) bottles sparkling water
Ice
2 limes, cut in thin slices
8 mint leaves

1. In a large pitcher, combine syrup, tequila, and sparkling water. Blend well.
2. Fill each glass with ice, and pour the punch over the ice.
3. Garnish each drink with one lime slice and one mint leaf.

Frozen Margarita

Frozen margaritas are magical. They seem to heighten the mood of any occasion. Blending the flavors of lime and tequila with the accent of salt and a hint of orange creates the perfect balance of flavor.

- 1 lime, cut into 6 wedges
- 1/4 tsp kosher or margarita salt
- 5 oz sugar-free lime-flavored syrup (such as Torani)
- 1/2 cup silver tequila
- 1 1/2 oz fresh-squeezed orange juice
- 5 cups cracked ice, divided use

1. Rub rim of each margarita glass with a lime wedge. Dust lightly with salt. Shake off any excess salt.
2. In blender, blend lime syrup, tequila, orange juice, and 3 cups ice until slushy, 2–3 minutes.
3. Add more ice, if desired. Pour into glasses and garnish each with a lime wedge.

Variation: To create the ultimate Frozen Margarita, drizzle each prepared margarita with 1 Tbsp sugar-free strawberry or raspberry syrup and garnish with 2–3 fresh strawberries or raspberries.

Tip

For a thicker frozen margarita, add more ice.

Serves: 6
Serving Size: About 8 oz
Prep Time: 15 minutes
Cook Time: N/A

Choices/Exchanges

1/2 Alcohol

Basic Nutritional Values

Calories	60
Calories from Fat	0
Total Fat	0.0 g
Saturated Fat	0.0 g
Trans Fat	0.0 g
Cholesterol	0 mg
Sodium	85 mg
Potassium	20 mg
Total Carbohydrate	1 g
Dietary Fiber	0 g
Sugars	1 g
Protein	0 g
Phosphorus	5 mg

Spicy Margarita

Serves: 1
Serving Size: 6 oz
Prep Time: 10 minutes
Cook Time: N/A

Choices/Exchanges

1/2 Carbohydrate,
1 Alcohol

Basic Nutritional Values

Calories	100
Calories from Fat	0
Total Fat	0.0 g
Saturated Fat	0.0 g
Trans Fat	0.0 g
Cholesterol	0 mg
Sodium	190 mg
Potassium	60 mg
Total Carbohydrate	5 g
Dietary Fiber	2 g
Sugars	3 g
Protein	0 g
Phosphorus	10 mg

Adding a sweet, spicy fruit flavor to the tartness of a margarita is a winning combination. The flavor lingers for a memorable margarita.

2 lime wedges
Salt
Cracked ice
1 oz silver tequila
1 Tbsp Sweet Chile Sauce (page 65)
1/2 cup liquid sugar-free margarita mix

1. If desired, rub rim of glass with lime and dust lightly with salt. Shake off any excess salt.
2. Fill glass half full of ice. Using a shaker, pour in tequila and Sweet Chile Sauce. Top with margarita mix. Shake and pour over ice.
3. Garnish with remaining lime wedge.

Fresco White Sangria

This white wine version of a Spanish favorite is refreshing and elegant. It is lighter than traditional sangria and not as sweet. I like to infuse the wine with a fruit-flavored syrup, adding a sweet, peachy flavor. Prepare this libation in a large pitcher a few hours before serving, so it takes on the natural accents and essence of sweetness from the fresh fruit.

- 1 (750-ml) bottle white wine, such as Pinot Grigio, Sauvignon Blanc, or Riesling
- 3 oz sugar-free peach-flavored syrup (such as Torani)
- 1 orange, thinly sliced
- 1 lemon, thinly sliced
- 1 peach, seeded, peeled, and diced
- 1 cup small seasonal berries (such as raspberries, or quartered and stemmed strawberries)
- 1 (1-L) bottle club soda or sparkling water

1. In a large pitcher, combine the wine and peach syrup. Add the orange slices, lemon slices, diced peaches, and seasonal berries. Refrigerate for 3 hours or overnight.
2. Pour wine goblets three-quarters full of the sangria, and top each glass with club soda or sparkling water.

Note: Medium to sweet white wine is a good selection for this sangria. However, a dry white wine—which has less sugar—also works well.

Serves: 10
Serving Size: 5 oz
Prep Time: 15 minutes
Chill Time: 3 hours up to 24 hours

Choices/Exchanges

1 Alcohol

Basic Nutritional Values

Calories	80
Calories from Fat	0
Total Fat	0.0 g
Saturated Fat	0.0 g
Trans Fat	0.0 g
Cholesterol	0 mg
Sodium	10 mg
Potassium	95 mg
Total Carbohydrate	4 g
Dietary Fiber	0 g
Sugars	2 g
Protein	0 g
Phosphorus	20 mg

Fruity Red Sangria

Serves: 8

Serving Size: 5 oz

Prep Time: 12 minutes

Chill Time: 3 hours up to 24 hours

Choices/Exchanges

1/2 Fruit, 1/2 Alcohol

Basic Nutritional Values

Calories	90
Calories from Fat	0
Total Fat	0.0 g
Saturated Fat	0.0 g
Trans Fat	0.0 g
Cholesterol	0 mg
Sodium	10 mg
Potassium	190 mg
Total Carbohydrate	7 g
Dietary Fiber	0 g
Sugars	4 g
Protein	0 g
Phosphorus	30 mg

Sangria is a spirited punch with Spanish origins. It is a combination of red wine, fresh fruit, and flavors of brandy or a hint of orange. A pretty glass pitcher or punch bowl filled with sangria will elevate any festive gathering.

1 (750-ml) bottle dry red wine, such as Merlot, Pinot Noir, or Zinfandel
Juice of 1 orange
Juice of 1 lemon
1 orange, thinly sliced
1 lemon, thinly sliced
2 cups seasonal berries (such as raspberries or diced strawberries)
2 cups sparkling water
Ice

1. In a large pitcher, combine wine, orange juice, and lemon juice. Add orange slices, lemon slices, and berries. Refrigerate overnight to ensure that the flavors infuse.
2. Just before serving, stir in the sparkling water. Pour over ice in individual glasses.

Michelada

This cool cocktail (pronounced *mee-chil-ahda*) is so refreshing! The combination of beer, lime juice, and ice cuts the calories and adds a citrusy flavor to my favorite drink, light beer.

Cracked ice
1/4 cup fresh-squeezed lime juice
1 bottle (12 oz) light beer (a light domestic or favorite Mexican beer)
1 or 2 lime slices

1. Fill a Collins glass or glass beer mug half full of ice.
2. Add the lime juice.
3. Slowly top with the beer to fill the glass.
4. Garnish with floating lime slices and serve.

Variation: Salt the rim of the glass margarita-style by rubbing the rim with lime and dusting it lightly with salt.

Serves: 1
Serving Size: 14 oz
Prep Time: 8 minutes
Cook Time: N/A

Choices/Exchanges

1/2 Carbohydrate,
1 Alcohol

Basic Nutritional Values

Calories	120
Calories from Fat	0
Total Fat	0.0 g
Saturated Fat	0.0 g
Trans Fat	0.0 g
Cholesterol	0 mg
Sodium	25 mg
Potassium	120 mg
Total Carbohydrate	10 g
Dietary Fiber	0 g
Sugars	1 g
Protein	1 g
Phosphorus	50 mg

Tequila Shots and Sangrita Chaser

Serves: 4
Serving Size: 4 1/4 oz
Prep Time: 12 minutes
Cook Time: N/A

Choices/Exchanges

1/2 Carbohydrate,
1 Alcohol

Basic Nutritional Values

Calories	100
Calories from Fat	0
Total Fat	0.0 g
Saturated Fat	0.0 g
Trans Fat	0.0 g
Cholesterol	0 mg
Sodium	40 mg
Potassium	200 mg
Total Carbohydrate	6 g
Dietary Fiber	0 g
Sugars	4 g
Protein	1 g
Phosphorus	20 mg

Taking a shot of tequila is a tradition in Tex-Mex hospitality. This little chaser was created to follow a shot of good tequila, enhancing the experience. *Sangrita* means "little blood" in Spanish.

1 cup low-sodium tomato juice
1/4 cup fresh-squeezed or low-sugar orange juice
1/4 cup fresh-squeezed lime juice
1 Tbsp sugar-free raspberry-flavored syrup (such as Torani)
1 tsp Worcestershire sauce
2 tsp hot pepper sauce
4 oz tequila

1. In a small pitcher, combine tomato juice, orange juice, lime juice, raspberry syrup, Worcestershire sauce, and hot pepper sauce. Mix well. Divide evenly between 4 small glasses.
2. Take a 1-oz shot of your favorite tequila. Then sip the Sangrita.

Note: For the hot pepper sauce, Louisiana Hot Sauce and Tabasco are good choices.

Paloma Fresco

Fresh fruit and tequila create the best cocktails! The freshness of grapefruit gives this drink a tart, sweet finish.

1 oz tequila
1/4 cup fresh grapefruit, peeled and diced with pith removed
Cracked ice
4 oz sugar-free grapefruit soda or grapefruit-flavored water
1 sprig mint

1. Pour tequila into highball glass. Add grapefruit. Muddle fruit and tequila together.
3. Fill the glass with ice, and top with soda or flavored water.
4. Garnish with mint.

Serves: 1
Serving Size: 5 oz
Prep Time: 12 minutes
Cook Time: N/A

Choices/Exchanges

1/2 Fruit, 1 Alcohol

Basic Nutritional Values

Calories	100
Calories from Fat	0
Total Fat	0.0 g
Saturated Fat	0.0 g
Trans Fat	0.0 g
Cholesterol	0 mg
Sodium	10 mg
Potassium	90 mg
Total Carbohydrate	5 g
Dietary Fiber	1 g
Sugars	4 g
Protein	0 g
Phosphorus	15 mg

Mexican Café

Serves: 4

Serving Size: 1 cup

Prep Time: 15 minutes

Cook Time: 2 minutes

Choices/Exchanges

1/2 Fat-Free Milk,
1/2 Carbohydrate

Basic Nutritional Values

Calories	90
Calories from Fat	0
Total Fat	0.0 g
Saturated Fat	0.1 g
Trans Fat	0.0 g
Cholesterol	0 mg
Sodium	55 mg
Potassium	250 mg
Total Carbohydrate	13 g
Dietary Fiber	0 g
Sugars	13 g
Protein	4 g
Phosphorus	130 mg

This simple composition of coffee and cream is actually a Spanish beverage enjoyed around the world.

2 cups fat-free milk
2 oz coffee liqueur
2 cups strong black coffee, heated to high temperature

1. In a small saucepan, heat milk over low heat until almost boiling.
2. Pour 1/2 cup milk into each mug, add 1/2 oz coffee liqueur, and top with 1/2 cup coffee.
3. Stir until well blended.

Mexican Hot Chocolate

This mug of goodness boasts the flavors of Mexican chocolate swirling in rich and creamy milk. The touch of cinnamon elevates this morning delight to a new level.

4 cups fat-free milk or milk substitute (see Note)
4 Tbsp unsweetened cocoa powder (such as Hershey's)
1 tsp ground cinnamon
1 tsp vanilla extract
1 tsp almond extract
Sugar substitute with sweetening equivalence of 2 Tbsp sugar
1 oz dark chocolate, grated

1. In a medium-sized saucepan, heat milk over medium-low heat.
2. Slowly add cocoa powder, cinnamon, vanilla and almond extracts, and sweetener.
3. Stir until well blended and heated through, 4–6 minutes. Garnish with grated dark chocolate.

Note: Dairy and milk products can add unwanted calories and fat to your diet. I like to use a variety of reduced-fat dairy products, such as almond milk, skim milk, and soy milk.

Serves: 4
Serving Size: 1 cup
Prep Time: 5 minutes
Cook Time: 10 minutes

Choices/Exchanges
1 Fat-Free Milk,
1/2 Carbohydrate

Basic Nutritional Values

Calories	150
Calories from Fat	25
Total Fat	3.0 g
Saturated Fat	1.9 g
Trans Fat	0.0 g
Cholesterol	5 mg
Sodium	105 mg
Potassium	510 mg
Total Carbohydrate	21 g
Dietary Fiber	3 g
Sugars	17 g
Protein	10 g
Phosphorus	305 mg

Bites and Starters

Starters and appetizers were not a tradition in Mexican cuisine. However, in the early 1900s, Tejanos (Texans of Spanish descent) developed multiple uses for the corn tortilla and started to serve warm, crispy corn tortilla chips and salsa in the little Tex-Mex cafés across Texas. This small culinary gesture became a phenomenon in dining out around the world. The creation of the crispy corn tortilla chip led to other favorites, like nachos and chile con queso served with chips. Light, healthy versions are easy to make and can help keep your blood glucose levels in balance without sacrificing flavor. Below is a tasty range of options for you to try.

Baked Crispy Corn Tortilla Chips 20

Pita Chips 21

Ceviche 22

Mini Shrimp Shooters. 23

Savory Mini Tostadas 24

Mini Hummus Tostaditos 25

Tex-Mex Nachos 26

Saucy Loaded Nachos. 27

Tres Quesos Street Nachos 28

Classic Guacamole. 29

Fresh Green Chile Guacamole 30

Charred Corn and Avocado Toss 31

Black Bean Layered Spread 32

Chile Bruschetta 33

Chile con Queso 35

Spinach and Artichoke Queso. 36

Mini Chimis. 37

Chile Pinwheels 38

Jalapeño Pinwheels 39

Roasted Green Chile Cheese Crisp 41

Quesadillas de Fresco. 42

Pineapple and Chile Quesadillas. 43

Chicken and Sweet Potato Quesadillas 44

Baked Crispy Corn Tortilla Chips

Serves: 6
Serving Size: 6 chips
Prep Time: 5 minutes
Cook Time: 16 minutes

Choices/Exchanges

1 Starch

Light and low-fat crispy tortilla chips can be whipped up in minutes. Adding different spices creates a nice variety for snacking.

> 6 (6-inch) Fresh Corn Tortillas (page 72), each cut into 6 wedges (see Tip for rounds)
> Cooking spray

1. Preheat oven to 400°F.
2. Spray tortilla wedges lightly with cooking spray, and sprinkle with salt (optional) or other spices.
3. Place on a baking sheet and bake until golden brown, turning once, 6–8 minutes per side.
4. Remove from baking sheet and serve immediately or let cool.

For later use: Store chips in an airtight container for up to 2 days. Serve them warm or at room temperature.

Basic Nutritional Values

Calories	60
Calories from Fat	10
Total Fat	1.0 g
Saturated Fat	0.1 g
Trans Fat	0.0 g
Cholesterol	0 mg
Sodium	95 mg
Potassium	45 mg
Total Carbohydrate	12 g
Dietary Fiber	2 g
Sugars	0 g
Protein	1 g
Phosphorus	35 mg

Tips

- For round chips, use a 2-inch round cookie cutter. Cut two 2-inch rounds out of each corn tortilla, discarding about 20% of each tortilla. Continue with Steps 1 and 2.
- Try a variety of spices, such as 1/4 tsp cumin, chili powder, or smoked chipotle.

Pita Chips

Pita chips are a flavorful change from corn tortilla chips. Baking whole-wheat pita bread slices is quick and easy. Create your favorite with flavored cooking sprays and additional spices.

4 whole-wheat pita bread pockets (see Note)
Cooking spray
1 tsp kosher salt

1. Preheat oven to 400°F. Slice each pita pocket into 6 wedges. Spray each wedge front and back with cooking spray. Season with salt.
2. Place wedges on a baking sheet. Bake 8–10 minutes, until crisp and golden brown.
3. Remove from baking sheet and serve immediately or let cool.

For later use: Store chips in an airtight container for up to 2 days. Serve them warm or at room temperature.

Note: For a thinner chip, separate each wedge into 2 pieces.

Serves: 24
Serving Size: 1 wedge
Prep Time: 6 minutes
Cook Time: 10 minutes

Choices/Exchanges

1/2 Starch

Basic Nutritional Values

Calories	35
Calories from Fat	10
Total Fat	1.0 g
Saturated Fat	0.2 g
Trans Fat	0.0 g
Cholesterol	0 mg
Sodium	130 mg
Potassium	15 mg
Total Carbohydrate	5 g
Dietary Fiber	1 g
Sugars	0 g
Protein	1 g
Phosphorus	15 mg

Ceviche

Serves: 8
Serving Size: 1/2 cup
Prep Time: 20 minutes
Cook Time: 6 minutes
Chill Time: 3 hours

Choices/Exchanges

1 Nonstarchy Vegetable,
2 Lean Protein

Basic Nutritional Values

Calories	100
Calories from Fat	15
Total Fat	1.5 g
Saturated Fat	0.2 g
Trans Fat	0.0 g
Cholesterol	20 mg
Sodium	160 mg
Potassium	530 mg
Total Carbohydrate	9 g
Dietary Fiber	2 g
Sugars	4 g
Protein	13 g
Phosphorus	160 mg

This Nuevo Tex-Mex starter is light and healthy. Fresh fish is accented with the acidity of fresh lime and teamed with cilantro and chile. Delicious when served with warm tortilla chips!

1 lb fresh or frozen (thawed) halibut, diced into bite-size pieces (see Tip)
Juice of 8–10 limes, divided use
1 medium onion, minced
4 tomatoes, seeded and finely chopped
2 fresh jalapeño peppers, seeded and minced
1 fresh yellow chile pepper, seeded and minced
2 cloves garlic, minced
1 Tbsp minced fresh cilantro
1/2 tsp kosher salt

1. Rinse fish and pat dry with a paper towel. Cut into 1/4-inch cubes
2. In a large bowl, toss fish and half the lime juice.
3. Coat a large skillet lightly with cooking spray. Over medium-high heat, gently sauté halibut and juice until firm and opaque, about 4–6 minutes. Using a food thermometer, cook fish to 145°F for food safety purposes. Remove from skillet with a slotted spoon and cool completely.
4. In a large bowl, gently combine cooked fish with remaining lime juice, onion, tomatoes, jalapeño and yellow chile peppers, garlic, and cilantro. Cover and refrigerate for 2–3 hours, stirring occasionally.
5. Just before serving, season with salt. Serve with Baked Crispy Corn Tortilla Chips (page 20) or Pita Chips (page 21).

Note: At times, there are concerns about the sustainability of some fish and seafood. Check reliable sites such as www.seachoice.org for the latest information.

Tip

You can use other firm-flesh fish, such as red snapper fillets, catfish, or tilapia.

Mini Shrimp Shooters

Shellfish is not typical Tex-Mex fare, but shrimp is always a great protein for a starter. This simple mini shrimp cocktail boasts chile and lime flavors that you will love—with fewer calories.

1/2 cup Tex-Mex Salsa (page 49) or store-bought tomato salsa in a brand of your choice
Juice of 2 medium limes
1 (11.5-oz) can low-sodium spicy vegetable juice
2 green onions, green part only, minced
1 lb (31–40 count) medium shrimp, cooked and peeled, chilled (see Tip)
6–12 sprigs cilantro

1. In a medium-sized bowl, combine salsa, lime juice, vegetable juice, and onions.
2. Add shrimp and toss until well coated.
3. Divide shrimp and salsa into eight shot glasses (about 4 shrimp per glass). Garnish with cilantro.

Serves: 8
Serving Size: About 1 1/2–2 oz
Prep Time: 20 minutes
Cook Time: N/A

Choices/Exchanges

1 Lean Protein

Basic Nutritional Values

Calories	50
Calories from Fat	0
Total Fat	0.0 g
Saturated Fat	0.0 g
Trans Fat	0.0 g
Cholesterol	60 mg
Sodium	230 mg
Potassium	230 mg
Total Carbohydrate	4 g
Dietary Fiber	1 g
Sugars	2 g
Protein	8 g
Phosphorus	90 mg

Tip

It is best to use fresh (never frozen) shrimp. If that is not possible, use shrimp that are free of preservatives (for example, shrimp that have not been treated with salt or STPP [sodium tripolyphosphate]).

Savory Mini Tostadas

Serves: 12
Serving Size: 1 tostada
Prep Time: 15 minutes
Cook Time: N/A

Choices/Exchanges

1 Starch, 1/2 Fat

Basic Nutritional Values

Calories	90
Calories from Fat	25
Total Fat	3.0 g
Saturated Fat	1.3 g
Trans Fat	0.0 g
Cholesterol	3 mg
Sodium	260 mg
Potassium	240 mg
Total Carbohydrate	12 g
Dietary Fiber	2 g
Sugars	1 g
Protein	5 g
Phosphorus	100 mg

These little tostadas are like tapas: bigger than a bite but smaller than a full tostada. Still, they are filling. The chip and beans create the foundation, piled high with freshness and spice.

1 cup Refried Beans (page 165) or store-bought reduced-fat refried beans, warmed
12 round baked corn tortilla chips, about 2 inches in diameter (see Tip in the recipe for Baked Crispy Corn Tortilla Chips, page 20)
4 oz shredded reduced-fat sharp cheddar cheese
1 cup chopped fresh spinach
1 cup chopped iceberg lettuce
1 tomato, seeded and chopped
2 green onions, thinly chopped
1 cup Tex-Mex Salsa (page 49)

1. Spread beans evenly on tortilla chips. Top each tostada with cheese, and place on a serving platter.
2. Top each tostada evenly with spinach, lettuce, tomato, and onions. Serve with salsa.

Tip

When I am rushed, I use store-bought fat-free refried beans.

Mini Hummus Tostaditos

Tostada is a Spanish word meaning "toast." In this recipe, *tostaditos* are the crispy little corn tortillas used as the foundation for this hand-held treat. The tortillas are spread with hummus and piled high with roasted peppers and crumbled cheese. These are a perfect snack or party appetizer and pair well with Fresco White Sangria (page 11) or Michelada (page 13).

> 1 cup plain hummus, a store-bought brand of your choice
> 12 round baked corn tortilla chips, about 2 inches in diameter (see Tip in the recipe for Baked Crispy Corn Tortilla Chips, page 20)
> 1 red bell pepper, roasted, seeded, peeled, and diced
> 1 cup shredded mixed greens
> 1/2 cup shredded reduced-fat Monterrey Jack, cheddar, or crumbled queso fresco and/or cotija cheese

1. Spread a thin layer of hummus on each chip, and place chips on a serving platter.
2. Top each chip with equal amounts of diced bell pepper, mixed greens, and cheese.

Variation: For green chile pesto tostaditos, spread the hummus on the chips, then spoon 1 tsp Green Chile Pesto (recipe below) on each chip. Top with equal amounts diced bell pepper, mixed greens, and cheese.

Green Chile Pesto: In a small bowl, combine 4 oz pesto (a store-bought brand of your choice) with 2 Tbsp chopped Roasted Green Chiles (page 152). Blend well, and serve at room temperature with chips or cocktail crackers.

Tip

Create your own low-carb baked corn tortilla chips with my recipe for Baked Crispy Corn Tortilla Chips (page 20).

Serves: 12
Serving Size: 1 tostadito
Prep Time: 12 minutes
Cook Time: N/A

Choices/Exchanges
1/2 Starch, 1/2 Fat

Basic Nutritional Values

Calories	80
Calories from Fat	30
Total Fat	3.5 g
Saturated Fat	0.9 g
Trans Fat	0.0 g
Cholesterol	4 mg
Sodium	180 mg
Potassium	95 mg
Total Carbohydrate	9 g
Dietary Fiber	2 g
Sugars	2 g
Protein	4 g
Phosphorus	75 mg

Tex-Mex Nachos

Serves: 12

Serving Size: 1 chip

Prep Time: 10 minutes

Cook Time: 2 minutes

Choices/Exchanges

1/2 Fat

Basic Nutritional Values

Calories	40
Calories from Fat	20
Total Fat	2.5 g
Saturated Fat	1.3 g
Trans Fat	0.0 g
Cholesterol	5 mg
Sodium	150 mg
Potassium	40 mg
Total Carbohydrate	3 g
Dietary Fiber	0 g
Sugars	0 g
Protein	3 g
Phosphorus	70 mg

History notes that nachos were created in the early 1940s when a group of military wives stopped in a small café along the southern Texas border. The maître d'—named Nacho—created a plate of fried corn tortilla chips topped with melted cheese and jalapeño strips. The ladies loved it and returned again and again for Nacho's Especial.

2 cups shredded iceberg lettuce, for garnish

12 Baked Crispy Corn Tortilla Chips (page 20) or a store-bought brand of your choice

1 1/2 cups shredded reduced-fat cheddar cheese

24 slices pickled jalapeños

1. Preheat broiler, with rack positioned 5–6 inches from heat element.
2. Spread lettuce on a serving platter, set aside.
3. Place the chips on an ovenproof platter, and top each chip equally with cheese and two jalapeño slices.
4. Broil until cheese is melted and bubbling, 1–2 minutes. Watch carefully so nachos do not burn!
5. Remove platter from broiler, and carefully move each nacho to the bed of lettuce. Serve immediately.

Saucy Loaded Nachos

Nachos are a true Tex-Mex tradition. Through the years they have taken on a life of their own with numerous variations. This light cheese sauce is a great foundation for your favorite nacho toppings.

8 oz lean ground beef or turkey (see Variation)
1/2 tsp cumin
1 cup chopped green onions (5–6 onions)
1 cup chopped red bell pepper
18 Baked Crispy Corn Tortilla Chips (page 20) or a store-bought brand of your choice
3/4 cup Classic Queso Sauce (page 54), warmed
1/3 cup pickled jalapeño pepper slices, drained
1/2 cup sliced black olives
1 medium tomato, seeded and diced
1 cup fat-free sour cream

1. Preheat oven to 200°F.
2. In a medium-sized skillet, cook meat over medium heat until browned and cooked through. Drain grease. Add cumin to meat, mix well, and set aside.
3. In the same skillet, sauté green onions and bell pepper over medium-low heat until soft, about 3 minutes. Set aside.
4. Place tortilla chips side by side on an ovenproof platter. Heat chips in the oven until warmed through, about 2 minutes. Remove chips from oven and drizzle with half the Queso Sauce. Set the rest of the Queso Sauce aside and keep it warm.
5. Top the chips with meat, onions, and bell pepper. Pour remaining Queso Sauce on top.
6. Garnish the nachos with jalapeños, olives, tomato, and sour cream.

Variation: For chicken or sirloin nachos, omit the ground beef, cumin, and salt, and add 12 oz cooked (lightly charred, cubed) chicken or sirloin.

Serves: 6
Serving Size: 3 chips
Prep Time: 20 minutes
Cook Time: 10 minutes

Choices/Exchanges

1/2 Starch, 1 Fat-Free Milk, 1 Nonstarchy Vegetable, 1 Lean Protein, 1/2 Fat

Basic Nutritional Values

Calories	230
Calories from Fat	80
Total Fat	9.0 g
Saturated Fat	4.2 g
Trans Fat	0.2 g
Cholesterol	40 mg
Sodium	470 mg
Potassium	450 mg
Total Carbohydrate	21 g
Dietary Fiber	3 g
Sugars	6 g
Protein	17 g
Phosphorus	340 mg

Tres Quesos Street Nachos

Serves: 8
Serving Size: 3 chips
Prep Time: 8 minutes
Cook Time: 10 minutes

Choices/Exchanges
1 Starch, 1/2 Fat

Basic Nutritional Values

Calories	100
Calories from Fat	45
Total Fat	5.0 g
Saturated Fat	2.5 g
Trans Fat	0.0 g
Cholesterol	15 mg
Sodium	250 mg
Potassium	110 mg
Total Carbohydrate	11 g
Dietary Fiber	2 g
Sugars	1 g
Protein	6 g
Phosphorus	135 mg

I like this unique blend of low-fat cheeses layered among crispy tortilla chips and topped with spices, produce, and fresh herbs.

1 cup corn kernels (see Tip)
1/4 cup drained and chopped pickled jalapeño pepper slices
1 Tbsp reduced-fat mayonnaise
1 tsp fresh-squeezed lime juice
24 Baked Crispy Corn Tortilla Chips (page 20) or a store-bought brand of your choice
1/2 cup shredded reduced-fat Monterey Jack cheese
1/2 cup shredded reduced-fat white cheddar cheese
1/4 cup crumbled cotija or feta cheese
1 Tbsp minced cilantro
3 green onions, green part only, diced

1. Spray a medium-sized skillet with cooking spray. Over medium heat, spread corn and jalapeño slices across the skillet. Cook until some of the kernels are popping and slightly charred. Remove from skillet. In a medium-sized bowl, toss corn with mayonnaise and lime juice. Set aside.
2. Place tortilla chips side by side on an ovenproof platter. Top evenly with cheeses, then with corn mixture. Broil until cheese is melted and chips are lightly toasted, about 4–6 minutes.
3. Remove from oven and sprinkle with cilantro and onions.

Tip

You can use frozen corn, thawed; cooked corn, cut from the cob; or canned corn, drained. For an added smoky flavor, use corn grilled on the barbecue grill.

Classic Guacamole

Guacamole has become a Tex-Mex party staple. Served with chips and salsa, it is a true crowd-pleaser. I like to serve it with jicama, radishes, and slices of red bell pepper. It is also a glorious garnish for so many Tex-Mex dishes, adding a rich natural flavor to our timeless favorites.

4 avocados, peeled and mashed
1 tomato, seeded and diced
1/4 cup minced onion
1/8 tsp pepper
1 Tbsp fresh-squeezed lime juice

1. In a large bowl, gently combine the avocados, tomato, and onion.
2. Add the pepper and lime juice, and mix well. Add salt to taste (if desired). Serve immediately.

For later use: Refrigerate in an airtight container for 30 minutes or for up to 2 hours.

Serves: 8
Serving Size: 2 Tbsp
Prep Time: 8 minutes
Cook Time: N/A

Choices/Exchanges

1 Fat

Basic Nutritional Values

Calories	50
Calories from Fat	40
Total Fat	4.5 g
Saturated Fat	0.7 g
Trans Fat	0.0 g
Cholesterol	0 mg
Sodium	0 mg
Potassium	180 mg
Total Carbohydrate	3 g
Dietary Fiber	2 g
Sugars	1 g
Protein	1 g
Phosphorus	20 mg

Fresh Green Chile Guacamole

Serves: 8
Serving Size: 2 Tbsp
Prep Time: 8 minutes
Cook Time: N/A

Choices/Exchanges

1/2 Fruit, 2 Fat

Basic Nutritional Values

Calories	120
Calories from Fat	100
Total Fat	11.0 g
Saturated Fat	1.6 g
Trans Fat	0.0 g
Cholesterol	0 mg
Sodium	80 mg
Potassium	380 mg
Total Carbohydrate	7 g
Dietary Fiber	5 g
Sugars	1 g
Protein	2 g
Phosphorus	40 mg

The smooth, buttery taste of avocados teamed with spicy green chiles adds a dimension of flavors that will grab your attention. Perfect for dipping Baked Crispy Corn Tortilla Chips (page 20), garnishing Seared Sirloin Tacos (page 112), or spreading on a Torta de Fresco Mexican Sandwich (page 149).

4 avocados, peeled and mashed
2 cloves garlic, minced
2 Tbsp Roasted Green Chiles, peeled and diced (page 152)
1 Tbsp fresh-squeezed lime juice
1/4 tsp salt

1. In a large bowl, gently combine the avocados, garlic, and chiles.
2. Add the lime juice and mix well. Add salt and blend well. Serve immediately.

For later use: Refrigerate in an airtight container for 30 minutes or for up to 2 hours.

Charred Corn and Avocado Toss

The fresh crispness of corn and the creaminess of avocado make this tasty medley satisfying.

Cooking spray
1 cup corn kernels (see Tip)
1/2 cup Roasted Green Chiles, peeled and diced (page 152)
1 Tbsp fresh-squeezed lime juice
1 Tbsp olive oil
1/4 tsp ground cumin
4 avocados, peeled and diced
1/16 tsp salt or salt substitute

1. Coat a medium-sized skillet with cooking spray.
2. Add the corn, and cook over medium-high heat until some of the kernels are popping and charred. Remove corn from skillet and let cool to room temperature.
3. In a medium-sized bowl, combine the corn with the green chiles, lime juice, olive oil, and cumin. Gently fold in avocado. Add salt to taste.
4. Serve immediately with crispy tortilla chips.

For later use: Refrigerate in an airtight container, stirring occasionally, for 30 minutes or for up to 2 hours. To serve, return to room temperature.

Serves: 12
Serving Size: 1/4 cup
Prep Time: 8 minutes
Cook Time: 4 minutes

Choices/Exchanges
1/2 Carbohydrate, 1 1/2 Fat

Basic Nutritional Values

Calories	100
Calories from Fat	80
Total Fat	9.0 g
Saturated Fat	1.2 g
Trans Fat	0.0 g
Cholesterol	0 mg
Sodium	15 mg
Potassium	300 mg
Total Carbohydrate	7 g
Dietary Fiber	4 g
Sugars	1 g
Protein	1 g
Phosphorus	40 mg

Tip

You can use frozen corn, thawed, or cooked corn, cut from the cob. For an added smoky flavor, use corn grilled on the barbecue grill.

Black Bean Layered Spread

Serves: 12
Serving Size: 3 chips and
   2 Tbsp spread
Prep Time: 14 minutes
Cook Time: N/A

Choices/Exchanges
1 Starch, 1/2 Fat-Free Milk,
1/2 Fat

Basic Nutritional Values

Calories	150
Calories from Fat	45
Total Fat	5.0 g
Saturated Fat	2.0 g
Trans Fat	0.0 g
Cholesterol	10 mg
Sodium	260 mg
Potassium	250 mg
Total Carbohydrate	20 g
Dietary Fiber	4 g
Sugars	2 g
Protein	8 g
Phosphorus	170 mg

This is my version of the classic seven-layer dip that originated in the 1980s—lighter and healthier thanks to reduced-fat cheeses and fat-free sour cream.

1 1/2 cups mashed black beans
1 1/2 cups fat-free sour cream
1 Tbsp low-sodium taco seasoning mix
1/2 cup Classic Guacamole (page 29)
1 1/3 cups shredded reduced-fat cheddar or Monterey Jack cheese
1 tomato, seeded and chopped
3 green onions, mostly green part, diced
1/2 cup sliced black olives
36 Baked Crispy Corn Tortilla Chips (page 20) or a store-bought brand of your choice

1. Spread beans evenly across the bottom of an 8 x 8-inch shallow serving dish or edged platter.
2. In a small bowl, combine sour cream and taco seasoning, and mix well. Spread over beans.
3. Top with layers of guacamole, cheese, tomato, onions, and olives. Serve with tortilla chips.

Chile Bruschetta

Olive oil–flavored toast topped with pungent garlic and fresh roasted chiles creates a marriage of unexpected flavors in this spicy appetizer. It is simple and delicious. I often use this green chile mixture as a relish on burgers, steak, and chicken.

1 small (8-oz) French whole-wheat/multigrain baguette loaf (see Tip)
Olive oil–flavored cooking spray
1 1/2 cups Roasted Green Chiles, peeled and diced (page 152)
4 cloves fresh garlic, minced
1/4 tsp kosher salt
2 Tbsp olive oil

1. Preheat oven to 400°F.
2. Slice bread into 32 slices, about 1/4 inch each. This should produce 30 to 36 slices.
3. Spray each slice lightly with cooking spray. Place on a baking sheet and bake until lightly browned on the edges and crispy, about 6–8 minutes.
4. Remove slices from baking sheet and cool to room temperature. Baguette slices will continue to harden as they cool.
5. In a medium-sized bowl, combine green chiles, garlic, kosher salt, and oil, mixing well.
6. Top each slice of bread with approximately 1 Tbsp chile mixture. Arrange on a platter and serve.

Tip
Look for whole-wheat baguettes at your local grocery store.

Serves: 8
Serving Size: 4 slices per serving
Prep Time: 14 minutes
Cook Time: 8 minutes

Choices/Exchanges
1 Starch, 1 Fat

Basic Nutritional Values

Calories	120
Calories from Fat	45
Total Fat	5.0 g
Saturated Fat	0.7 g
Trans Fat	0.0 g
Cholesterol	0 mg
Sodium	210 mg
Potassium	190 mg
Total Carbohydrate	16 g
Dietary Fiber	2 g
Sugars	2 g
Protein	3 g
Phosphorus	90 mg

Chile con Queso, p. 35; Spinach and Artichoke Queso, p. 36

Chile con Queso

Another Tex-Mex classic! A combination of hot chiles and rich cheeses have made this a tasty garnish and appetizer around the world. Using reduced-fat cheese greatly reduces the fat in my queso.

2 cloves garlic, minced
3 Tbsp Roasted Green Chiles, peeled and diced (page 152)
2 Tbsp reduced-sodium chicken stock
2 cups (about 8 oz) shredded reduced-fat cheddar cheese
4 oz white or yellow processed cheese (such as Velveeta), cubed
3 Tbsp skim milk
2 Tbsp hot sauce (see Note)
1 Tbsp cilantro
1 medium tomato, seeded and chopped

1. In a small saucepan, sauté garlic and green chiles in stock over medium-low heat until garlic is soft, about 2 minutes.
2. Add cheeses and milk, stirring until well blended.
3. Immediately pour into a serving dish. Drizzle hot sauce across the top.
4. Garnish with cilantro and chopped tomato.

Note: For the hot sauce, select a store-bought brand of your choice. Cholula and Tabasco heighten the taste of this queso.

Variation: For a spicier queso, add 1/2 cup Tex-Mex Salsa (page 49) in Step 1.

Serves: 32
Serving Size: 1 Tbsp
Prep Time: 8 minutes
Cook Time: 6 minutes

Choices/Exchanges
1/2 Fat

Basic Nutritional Values

Calories	30
Calories from Fat	20
Total Fat	2.0 g
Saturated Fat	1.2 g
Trans Fat	0.0 g
Cholesterol	5 mg
Sodium	120 mg
Potassium	35 mg
Total Carbohydrate	1 g
Dietary Fiber	0 g
Sugars	1 g
Protein	2 g
Phosphorus	75 mg

Spinach and Artichoke Queso

Serves: 32
Serving Size: 1 Tbsp
Prep Time: 8 minutes
Cook Time: 10 minutes

Choices/Exchanges

1/2 Fat

Basic Nutritional Values

Calories	30
Calories from Fat	20
Total Fat	2.0 g
Saturated Fat	1.1 g
Trans Fat	0.0 g
Cholesterol	5 mg
Sodium	125 mg
Potassium	30 mg
Total Carbohydrate	1 g
Dietary Fiber	0 g
Sugars	0 g
Protein	2 g
Phosphorus	75 mg

Adding fresh veggies for fullness and texture creates a delicious and colorful queso. The creamy garlicky goodness is fresh and tasty.

2 cloves garlic, crushed
1 tsp olive oil
1/4 cup chopped spinach
1/4 cup chopped artichoke hearts
3 Tbsp unsweetened almond milk
1 1/2 cups (about 6 oz) shredded reduced-fat white American cheese
4 oz white processed cheese (such as Velveeta Blanca)

1. In a medium-sized skillet, sauté garlic in olive oil over medium heat until garlic is soft, about 2 minutes.
2. Add spinach and artichoke hearts and sauté until heated soft and cooked through, 3–4 minutes.
3. Slowly add milk and stir in cheeses. Reduce heat and cook until well blended.
4. Immediately pour into a serving dish, and serve with chips or warmed corn tortillas.

Mini Chimis

These little chimichangas are a hearty favorite. Baking the little burrito gems lightens them up to make a healthy version. The crispy flour tortilla wrapped around a tasty filling makes the perfect appetizer for dipping. Serve with queso, guacamole, and fat-free sour cream.

1 1/2 cups Shredded Beef (page 153)
1/4 tsp salt
6 (8-inch) Fresh Whole-Grain Flour Tortillas (page 70)
Cooking spray

1. In a medium-sized bowl, combine meat and salt, mixing well.
2. To build the chimichangas, place 1/4 cup beef filling at one end of each tortilla. Fold the tortilla in on both sides to cover the filling, then gently roll the tortilla all the way up and secure with a toothpick. Place rolled chimichangas in a resealable plastic bag to set and keep moist.
3. When ready to bake, preheat oven to 375°F. Spray each chimichanga lightly with cooking spray, and place seam side down on a baking sheet. Bake until they start to brown, 12–16 minutes. Turn each chimichanga over and bake for 8 minutes more, until golden brown and crispy.
4. To serve, gently cut each chimichanga in half at an angle with a sharp knife. Place on a serving platter with a side of Tex-Mex Salsa (page 49) and Classic Guacamole (page 29).

Variations:

- Omit beef and add 1 1/2 cups Shredded Chicken (page 155). Follow Steps 1–4.
- For a lighter version, omit beef and divide 1 1/2 cups Refried Beans (page 165) and 1 cup (about 4 oz) shredded reduced-fat cheddar cheese evenly among the tortillas. Follow Steps 1–4.

Serves: 12
Serving Size: 1/2 chimichanga
Prep Time: 12 minutes
Cook Time: 16 minutes

Choices/Exchanges
1 Starch, 1 Lean Protein, 1/2 Fat

Basic Nutritional Values

Calories	130
Calories from Fat	40
Total Fat	4.5 g
Saturated Fat	0.9 g
Trans Fat	0.1 g
Cholesterol	25 mg
Sodium	240 mg
Potassium	140 mg
Total Carbohydrate	11 g
Dietary Fiber	1 g
Sugars	0 g
Protein	10 g
Phosphorus	105 mg

Chile Pinwheels

Serves: 16
Serving Size: 2 pinwheels
Prep Time: 8 minutes
Chill Time: 2 hours

Choices/Exchanges

1/2 Starch, 1/2 Fat

Basic Nutritional Values

Calories	60
Calories from Fat	35
Total Fat	4.0 g
Saturated Fat	1.7 g
Trans Fat	0.0 g
Cholesterol	10 mg
Sodium	140 mg
Potassium	60 mg
Total Carbohydrate	5 g
Dietary Fiber	1 g
Sugars	1 g
Protein	2 g
Phosphorus	35 mg

These simple creamy bites are filled with flavor. Whole-wheat tortillas and reduced-fat cream cheese create a healthy little starter. Make ahead, and chill until ready to serve.

8 oz reduced-fat cream cheese
1/2 cup Roasted Green Chiles, peeled and diced (page 152)
1/2 tsp garlic salt
4 (8-inch) Fresh Whole-Grain Flour Tortillas (page 70)
1 Tbsp minced cilantro or flat-leaf parsley

1. In a medium-sized bowl, combine cream cheese, chiles, and garlic salt. Blend well. Spread 4 Tbsp filling to the outer edge of each tortilla, covering the full surface.
2. Roll tortilla up tightly, making sure each tortilla ends as an evenly round tube shape. Place the rolled tortillas in a large resealable plastic bag. Seal the bag, and refrigerate for 2–3 hours or overnight.
3. To serve, slice each tortilla into 8 rounds (about 1/4 inch each), discarding the ends. Arrange rounds on a platter. Sprinkle the filled platter with cilantro or parsley.

Jalapeño Pinwheels

8 oz reduced-fat cream cheese
1 green onion, green part only, minced
3 Tbsp minced red bell pepper
1 jalapeño, seeded and minced
1/2 tsp kosher salt
4 (8-inch) Fresh Whole-Grain Flour Tortillas (page 70)

1. In a medium-sized bowl, combine cream cheese, onion, bell pepper, jalapeño, and salt. Blend well. Spread 4 Tbsp filling to the outer edge of each tortilla, covering the full surface.
2. Roll tortilla up tightly, making sure each tortilla ends as an evenly round tube shape. Place the rolled tortillas in a large resealable plastic bag. Seal the bag, and refrigerate for 2–3 hours or overnight.
3. To serve, slice each tortilla into 8 rounds (about 1/4 inch each), discarding the ends. Arrange on a platter.

Serves: 16
Serving Size: 2 pinwheels
Prep Time: 8 minutes
Chill Time: 2 hours

Choices/Exchanges
1/2 Starch, 1/2 Fat

Basic Nutritional Values

Calories	60
Calories from Fat	35
Total Fat	4.0 g
Saturated Fat	1.7 g
Trans Fat	0.0 g
Cholesterol	10 mg
Sodium	130 mg
Potassium	55 mg
Total Carbohydrate	5 g
Dietary Fiber	1 g
Sugars	1 g
Protein	2 g
Phosphorus	35 mg

Roasted Green Chile Cheese Crisp

I love a simple cheese crisp: a toasted flour tortilla topped with melted cheese and a bit of chile. Sliced and served like a pizza, it's a crowd favorite. The combination of chile, cheese, and butter has a distinct flavor that reminds me of growing up on the Texas–Mexico border.

Butter-flavored cooking spray
1 (10-inch) Fresh Whole-Grain Flour Tortilla (page 71)
1 cup (about 4 oz) shredded reduced-fat cheddar cheese
2 Tbsp Roasted Green Chiles (page 152)

1. Preheat broiler, with rack positioned 3-4 inches from heat element.
2. Lightly spray one side of tortilla with cooking spray to edges of tortilla. Place tortilla, sprayed side up, on a baking sheet, and spread cheese and chiles evenly across tortilla.
3. Broil tortilla until cheese is melted and tortilla is crispy around the edges and slightly brown, 2-3 minutes. Slice into 6 wedges.

Serves: 6
Serving Size: 1 wedge
Prep Time: 8 minutes
Cook Time: 3 minutes

Choices/Exchanges

1/2 Starch, 1 Fat

Basic Nutritional Values

Calories	90
Calories from Fat	45
Total Fat	5.0 g
Saturated Fat	2.5 g
Trans Fat	0.0 g
Cholesterol	10 mg
Sodium	180 mg
Potassium	65 mg
Total Carbohydrate	6 g
Dietary Fiber	1 g
Sugars	0 g
Protein	6 g
Phosphorus	135 mg

Quesadillas de Fresco

Serves: 6
Serving Size: 1 wedge
Prep Time: 5 minutes
Cook Time: 6 minutes

Choices/Exchanges

1 Starch, 1 Fat

Basic Nutritional Values

Calories	130
Calories from Fat	60
Total Fat	7.0 g
Saturated Fat	2.6 g
Trans Fat	0.0 g
Cholesterol	15 mg
Sodium	230 mg
Potassium	160 mg
Total Carbohydrate	14 g
Dietary Fiber	2 g
Sugars	1 g
Protein	7 g
Phosphorus	145 mg

Fresh vegetables wrapped in warm melted cheese makes this quesadilla a favorite. I use a simple Pico de Gallo, but any combination of finely chopped vegetables will add freshness.

Cooking spray
2 (10-inch) Fresh Whole-Grain Flour Tortillas (page 71)
1 cup (about 4 oz) shredded reduced-fat Monterey Jack or cheddar cheese
1/2 cup Pico de Gallo (page 48), drained

1. Coat a large skillet lightly with cooking spray.
2. Place one tortilla in the skillet, and cook over medium heat until air bubbles begin to form, about 1 minute.
3. Spread half the cheese evenly over the tortilla, covering to the edges. Spread half the Pico de Gallo over the cheese. Cook until the cheese starts to melt, about 1 minute.
4. Fold tortilla in half to create a half-moon shape. Flip folded tortilla over, and cook until tortilla is lightly toasted and cheese filling is completely melted, 1–2 minutes.
5. Transfer quesadilla to a cutting board. Recoat the skillet with cooking spray, and repeat with second tortilla and remaining cheese and Pico de Gallo.
6. Cut each quesadilla into 3 wedges, and serve immediately with Classic Guacamole (page 29).

Pineapple and Chile Quesadillas

Multiple layers of flavor, from sweet to savory, make this quesadilla so inviting. The pepper flakes add heat and a spicy goodness.

Cooking spray
1/2 cup small pineapple chunks, drained
2 (10-inch) Fresh Whole-Grain Flour Tortillas (page 71)
1 cup (about 4 oz) shredded reduced-fat Monterey Jack or white cheddar cheese
1 tsp crushed red pepper flakes

1. Coat a large skillet lightly with cooking spray.
2. Chop pineapple into bite-size pieces and cook over medium-high heat until lightly charred. Remove from skillet and set aside.
3. Recoat the skillet with cooking spray. Place one tortilla in the skillet, and cook over medium heat until air bubbles begin to form, about 1 minute.
4. Spread half the cheese evenly over the tortilla, covering to the edges. Top the cheese-covered tortilla with half the pineapple. Sprinkle with half the red pepper flakes. Cook until the cheese starts to melt, about 1 minute.
5. Fold tortilla in half to create a half-moon shape. Flip folded tortilla over, and cook until tortilla is lightly toasted and cheese filling is completely melted, 1–2 minutes.
6. Transfer quesadilla to a cutting board. Recoat the skillet with cooking spray, and repeat with second tortilla and remaining cheese, pineapple, and red pepper flakes.
7. Cut each quesadilla into 3 wedges, and serve hot with Roasted Tomatillo Chile Sauce (page 50).

Serves: 6
Serving Size: 1 wedge
Prep Time: 3 minutes
Cook Time: 10 minutes

Choices/Exchanges

1 Starch, 1 Fat

Basic Nutritional Values

Calories. 130
Calories from Fat 60
Total Fat . . . . 7.0 g
Saturated Fat . . . . 2.6 g
Trans Fat . . . . 0.0 g
Cholesterol . . . . 15 mg
Sodium . . . . 210 mg
Potassium . . . . 95 mg
Total Carbohydrate. . . . . . . 14 g
Dietary Fiber . . . . 2 g
Sugars. . . . . 2 g
Protein . . . . .7 g
Phosphorus . . . . .135 mg

Chicken and Sweet Potato Quesadillas

Serves: 6
Serving Size: 1 wedge
Prep Time: 12 minutes
Cook Time: 6 minutes

Choices/Exchanges

1 Starch, 2 Lean Protein,
1/2 Fat

Basic Nutritional Values

Calories	200
Calories from Fat	60
Total Fat	7.0 g
Saturated Fat	2.3 g
Trans Fat	0.0 g
Cholesterol	40 mg
Sodium	250 mg
Potassium	210 mg
Total Carbohydrate	16 g
Dietary Fiber	3 g
Sugars	2 g
Protein	18 g
Phosphorus	195 mg

The sweetness of the potato highlights the savory chicken and cheese in this quesadilla. This unusual combination is irresistible.

Cooking spray
2 (10-inch) Fresh Whole-Grain Flour Tortillas (page 71)
3/4 cup (about 3 oz) shredded reduced-fat Monterey Jack or white cheddar cheese
1 small sweet potato (about 1/2 cup), cooked, peeled, and mashed
1 cup Shredded Chicken (page 155)
1/8 tsp salt

1. Coat a large skillet lightly with cooking spray.
2. Place one tortilla in the skillet and cook over medium heat until air bubbles begin to form, about 1 minute.
3. Spread half the cheese evenly over the tortilla, covering to the edges. As the cheese is melting, top with half the sweet potato, then half the chicken. Season with half the salt.
4. Fold tortilla in half to create a half-moon shape. Flip folded tortilla over, and cook until tortilla is lightly toasted and cheese filling is completely melted, 1–2 minutes.
5. Transfer quesadilla to a cutting board. Recoat the skillet with cooking spray, and repeat with second tortilla and remaining cheese, sweet potato, chicken, and salt.
6. Cut each quesadilla into 3 wedges, and serve immediately with Spicy Corn Salsa (page 52).

Salsas and More

This collection of salsas and sauces brings big flavors together, enhancing the flavor of grilled meats and poultry, lacing the edges of tacos, and saucing cheesy enchiladas. Infusing sweet, spicy, and savory splashes of sauce and delicate salsas into Tex-Mex recipes accents these authentic and traditional dishes with tangy, creamy, spicy, citrusy, rich, refreshing flavors.

Pico de Gallo 48

Tex-Mex Salsa. 49

Roasted Tomatillo Chile Sauce 50

Citrusy Salsa 51

Spicy Corn Salsa 52

Mexican White Sauce 53

Classic Queso Sauce 54

Pickled Onions 55

Roasted Pineapple Salsa 57

Coleslaw Relish. 58

Jicama Salsa. 59

Chile Cream Sauce. 60

Tex-Mex Chile Gravy 61

Fresh Veggie Enchilada Sauce 62

Red Enchilada Sauce 63

Green Chile Enchilada Sauce 64

Sweet Chile Sauce 65

Sidebar:

   Red Chile Purée 66

Pico de Gallo

- -

Serves: 16
Serving Size: 2 Tbsp
Prep Time: 30 minutes
Chill Time: 1 hour

Choices/Exchanges

1 Nonstarchy Vegetable

Basic Nutritional Values

Calories	15
Calories from Fat	0
Total Fat	0.0 g
Saturated Fat	0.0 g
Trans Fat	0.0 g
Cholesterol	0 mg
Sodium	35 mg
Potassium	130 mg
Total Carbohydrate	3 g
Dietary Fiber	1 g
Sugars	2 g
Protein	1 g
Phosphorus	15 mg

This salsa has a crisp, refreshing flavor that captures the true essence of Mexico! The combination of fresh tomatoes and chiles accented with cilantro and onion is irresistible.

> 4 medium (about 6 oz each) tomatoes, seeded and diced
> 3 jalapeño peppers, seeded and minced
> 1 serrano chile pepper, seeded and minced
> 1 medium (6-oz) onion, finely chopped
> 2 Tbsp minced fresh cilantro
> Juice of 1 lime
> 1/4 tsp kosher salt

1. Combine tomatoes, jalapeños, serrano chile, onion, and cilantro in a large bowl.
2. Add lime juice and mix well. Cover and refrigerate, stirring occasionally, for 1 hour or up to 24 hours.
3. Add salt to taste just before serving.

Tex-Mex Salsa

This table salsa is a mainstay at our house. Simple to make, it goes well with tacos and enchiladas as well as grilled chicken and steak. The combination of fresh and canned ingredients works well for a tried and true recipe. I also love it piled high on a crisp corn tortilla chip!

1 (28-oz) can low-sodium diced tomatoes (see Note)
1 medium onion, chopped
1/4 cup Roasted Green Chiles, peeled and diced (page 152)
1 clove garlic, minced
1 Tbsp crushed red pepper flakes
1/2 tsp kosher salt

1. Combine tomatoes, onion, green chiles, and garlic in a large bowl. Mix well.
2. Blend in red pepper flakes and salt.
3. Refrigerate in an airtight container for 1 hour or for up to 24 hours.

Note: For a smoother salsa, process tomatoes in food processor for 1–2 minutes.

Variation: For more Tex-Mex flavor, add 1 tsp cumin.

Serves: 28
Serving Size: 2 Tbsp
Prep Time: 15 minutes
Chill Time: 1 hour

Choices/Exchanges

Free food

Basic Nutritional Values

Calories	10
Calories from Fat	0
Total Fat	0.0 g
Saturated Fat	0.0 g
Trans Fat	0.0 g
Cholesterol	0 mg
Sodium	45 mg
Potassium	70 mg
Total Carbohydrate	2 g
Dietary Fiber	0 g
Sugars	1 g
Protein	0 g
Phosphorus	10 mg

Roasted Tomatillo Chile Sauce

Serves: 16

Serving Size: 2 Tbsp

Prep Time: 12 minutes

Cook Time: 7 minutes

Chill Time: 1 hour

Choices/Exchanges

Free food

Basic Nutritional Values

Calories	10
Calories from Fat	0
Total Fat	0.0 g
Saturated Fat	0.0 g
Trans Fat	0.0 g
Cholesterol	0 mg
Sodium	35 mg
Potassium	95 mg
Total Carbohydrate	2 g
Dietary Fiber	1 g
Sugars	1 g
Protein	0 g
Phosphorus	15 mg

This sauce has a unique flavor: citrusy charred tomatillos teamed with a hint of chile. (Tomatillos, a member of the tomato family, are grown in many Texas gardens.) The charred or slightly blackened skins of the roasted tomatillos will enrich your sauces with a smoky flavor.

6 fresh tomatillos (about 3 oz each)
1/4 cup Roasted Green Chiles, peeled and diced (page 152)
2 cloves garlic, peeled
1/2 tsp salt or salt substitute

1. Preheat broiler, with rack positioned 1–2 inches from heat element.
2. Remove husks from the tomatillos, and rinse under warm water to remove stickiness.
3. Broil tomatillos, turning once, until tomatillos are softened and slightly charred, about 7 minutes. Remove from oven and cool to room temperature.
4. Place green chiles, garlic, salt, and tomatillos in food processor. Purée all ingredients until just slightly chunky.
5. Refrigerate in an airtight container for 1 hour or for up to 24 hours.

Citrusy Salsa

Adding good fiber that is sweet and spicy in a salsa is a real treat. This salsa teams well with creamy quesadillas and heightens the taste of fish and chicken tacos.

4 medium oranges, peeled and sectioned, pith removed
3 limes, peeled and sectioned, pith removed
1 jalapeño pepper, seeded and chopped
2 green onions, green part only, chopped
1 tsp crushed red pepper flakes

1. Cut orange and lime sections into small chunks and place in a large bowl.
2. Add jalapeño, onions, and red pepper flakes. Mix well.
3. Refrigerate in an airtight container for 1 hour or for up to 24 hours.

Serves: 16
Serving Size: 2 Tbsp
Prep Time: 15 minutes
Chill Time: 1 hour

Choices/Exchanges

1/2 Fruit

Basic Nutritional Values

Calories	25
Calories from Fat	0
Total Fat	0.0 g
Saturated Fat	0.0 g
Trans Fat	0.0 g
Cholesterol	0 mg
Sodium	0 mg
Potassium	100 mg
Total Carbohydrate	6 g
Dietary Fiber	1 g
Sugars	4 g
Protein	1 g
Phosphorus	10 mg

Spicy Corn Salsa

Serves: 16
Serving Size: 2 Tbsp
Prep Time: 6 minutes
Chill Time: 1 hour

Choices/Exchanges
Free food

This hearty salsa has a great depth of flavor and a crisp and crunchy texture. Plus, just a spoonful will give you added fiber and vitamins—but no added fat, sugar, or sodium.

1 1/2 cups corn kernels, cooked, drained
Juice of 3 medium-sized limes (about 1/4 cup)
1/4 cup minced red onion
2 green onions, green part only, minced
2 tsp minced fresh cilantro
1/2 tsp crushed red pepper flakes

1. In a large bowl, combine corn, lime juice, onions, and cilantro. Mix well. Add red pepper flakes, and season with salt (if desired).
2. Refrigerate in an airtight container, stirring occasionally, for 1 hour or for up to 2 days.

Basic Nutritional Values

Calories	15
Calories from Fat	0
Total Fat	0.0 g
Saturated Fat	0.0 g
Trans Fat	0.0 g
Cholesterol	0 mg
Sodium	0 mg
Potassium	50 mg
Total Carbohydrate	3 g
Dietary Fiber	0 g
Sugars	1 g
Protein	1 g
Phosphorus	15 mg

Mexican White Sauce

This light tangy sauce is the perfect finish for so many Tex-Mex dishes. Just a drizzle gives tacos, tostadas, and enchiladas an added burst of creamy flavor.

3/4 cup reduced-fat mayonnaise
1/2 cup fat-free plain yogurt
2 Tbsp fresh-squeezed lime juice (about 1 lime)

1. In a medium-sized bowl, combine mayonnaise and yogurt. Add lime juice and whisk until smooth.
2. Refrigerate in an airtight container or squeeze bottle, stirring occasionally, for 1 hour or for up to 4 days.

Variation: Customize this sauce by adding any of the following: 1/2 tsp chili powder, 1/2 tsp cumin, or 1 tsp fresh minced cilantro.

Serves: 16
Serving Size: 1 Tbsp
Prep Time: 2 minutes
Chill Time: 1 hour

Choices/Exchanges

1/2 Fat

Basic Nutritional Values

Calories	35
Calories from Fat	25
Total Fat	3.0 g
Saturated Fat	0.4 g
Trans Fat	0.0 g
Cholesterol	3 mg
Sodium	95 mg
Potassium	20 mg
Total Carbohydrate	2 g
Dietary Fiber	0 g
Sugars	1 g
Protein	0 g
Phosphorus	15 mg

Classic Queso Sauce

Serves: 24
Serving Size: 1 Tbsp
Prep Time: 8 minutes
Cook Time: 10 minutes

Choices/Exchanges

1 Fat

Basic Nutritional Values

Calories	40
Calories from Fat	20
Total Fat	2.0 g
Saturated Fat	1.4 g
Trans Fat	0.0 g
Cholesterol	5 mg
Sodium	120 mg
Potassium	45 mg
Total Carbohydrate	2 g
Dietary Fiber	0 g
Sugars	1 g
Protein	3 g
Phosphorus	100 mg

This classic sauce can be used in so many ways. It's great as a dipping sauce for fresh veggies or on grilled chicken or beef. Or my favorite: poured over crispy chips, then topped with nacho garnishes.

1 Tbsp butter
1 clove garlic
1 cup fat-free half-and-half
1/4 tsp onion powder
1/4 tsp garlic powder
1/4 tsp white pepper
4 oz reduced-fat or 2% processed cheese, cut in cubes
1 1/2 cups (about 6 oz) shredded reduced-fat sharp cheddar cheese

1. In a medium-sized saucepan, melt butter and garlic together over medium-low heat.
2. Add half-and-half and spices, stirring constantly.
3. Reduce heat to low and slowly add cheeses. Blend until cheeses are melted. Continue stirring until the mixture thickens. Serve warm.

Pickled Onions

This zesty garnish, a Tex-Mex favorite, is perfect for tacos and enchiladas and is so easy to make.

1 medium red onion, thinly sliced
1/2 cup fresh-squeezed lime juice (about 4 limes)
3/4 tsp salt

1. Place onion in a medium-sized bowl. Pour boiling water over onion until covered.
2. Immediately rinse onions through a strainer, shake off excess water, and return to bowl.
3. Add lime juice and salt. Mix well.
4. Refrigerate in an airtight container for 1 hour or for up to 4 days.

Serves: 16
Serving Size: 1 Tbsp
Prep Time: 3 minutes
Chill Time: 1 hour

Choices/Exchanges
Free food

Basic Nutritional Values

Calories	5
Calories from Fat	0
Total Fat	0.0 g
Saturated Fat	0.0 g
Trans Fat	0.0 g
Cholesterol	0 mg
Sodium	110 mg
Potassium	20 mg
Total Carbohydrate	1 g
Dietary Fiber	0 g
Sugars	1 g
Protein	0 g
Phosphorus	5 mg

Pickled Onions, p. 55; Roasted Pineapple Salsa, p. 57; Roasted Tomatillo Chile Sauce, p. 50; Mexican White Sauce, p. 53

Roasted Pineapple Salsa

This sweet, spicy combination is especially tasty on warm tortilla chips.

2 cups drained and chopped pineapple chunks
1/4 cup minced red onion
1/4 cup diced red bell pepper
1 jalapeño pepper, seeded and minced
3 green onions, green part only, chopped

1. In a skillet over high heat, cook pineapple chunks until slightly charred, about 2 minutes. Remove from skillet and cool to room temperature.
2. Place pineapple chunks in a large bowl. Add onion, bell pepper, jalapeño, and green onions. Mix well.
3. Refrigerate in an airtight container, stirring occasionally, for 1 hour or for up to 24 hours.

Serves: 20
Serving Size: 2 Tbsp
Prep Time: 6 minutes
Cook Time: 2 minutes
Chill Time: 1 hour

Choices/Exchanges

Free food

Basic Nutritional Values

Calories	15
Calories from Fat	0
Total Fat	0.0 g
Saturated Fat	0.0 g
Trans Fat	0.0 g
Cholesterol	0 mg
Sodium	0 mg
Potassium	40 mg
Total Carbohydrate	3 g
Dietary Fiber	0 g
Sugars	3 g
Protein	0 g
Phosphorus	5 mg

Coleslaw Relish

Serves: 10
Serving Size: 1/4 cup
Prep Time: 12 minutes
Chill Time: 2 hours

Choices/Exchanges

1 Fat

Basic Nutritional Values

Calories	60
Calories from Fat	50
Total Fat	6.0 g
Saturated Fat	0.4 g
Trans Fat	0.0 g
Cholesterol	0 mg
Sodium	120 mg
Potassium	40 mg
Total Carbohydrate	2 g
Dietary Fiber	1 g
Sugars	1 g
Protein	0 g
Phosphorus	5 mg

This Tex-Mex relish is tangy and delicious. I often serve it with Pork Carnitas Tacos (page 114) or as a garnish with various Tex-Mex entrees such as South Texas Fish Tacos (page 126).

1/4 cup canola oil
3 Tbsp white vinegar
1/2 tsp salt
2 1/2 cups shredded green cabbage
1/2 medium onion, grated

1. In a medium-sized bowl, combine oil, vinegar, and salt.
2. Slowly fold in cabbage and onion, and toss until they are well coated.
3. Refrigerate in an airtight container for 2 hours up to 6 hours so the coleslaw will marinate completely.

Jicama Salsa

Jicama is a crunchy-textured root vegetable that takes on other flavors well. This salsa adds volume and a tangy, spicy flavor to tacos and burritos.

1 cup peeled, diced jicama
1/2 cup diced red onion
1/3 cup fresh-squeezed lemon juice (about 3 lemons)
1 tsp minced flat-leaf parsley
1 tsp crushed red pepper flakes
1/2 tsp salt

1. Place jicama, onion, and lemon juice in a large bowl. Mix well.
2. Add parsley, red pepper flakes, and salt, and stir.
3. Refrigerate in an airtight container for 1 hour or for up to 24 hours.

Serves: 12
Serving Size: 2 Tbsp
Prep Time: 12 minutes
Chill Time: 1 hour

Choices/Exchanges

Free food

Basic Nutritional Values

Calories	10
Calories from Fat	0
Total Fat	0.0 g
Saturated Fat	0.0 g
Trans Fat	0.0 g
Cholesterol	0 mg
Sodium	100 mg
Potassium	35 mg
Total Carbohydrate	2 g
Dietary Fiber	1 g
Sugars	1 g
Protein	0 g
Phosphorus	5 mg

Chile Cream Sauce

Serves: 21
Serving Size: 1 Tbsp
Prep Time: 8 minutes
Cook Time: N/A

Choices/Exchanges

1/2 Fat

Basic Nutritional Values

Calories	20
Calories from Fat	15
Total Fat	1.5 g
Saturated Fat	0.2 g
Trans Fat	0.0 g
Cholesterol	0 mg
Sodium	135 mg
Potassium	20 mg
Total Carbohydrate	1 g
Dietary Fiber	0 g
Sugars	1 g
Protein	0 g
Phosphorus	10 mg

A dollop of this sauce can completely change Huevos Rancheros (page 81) or a steamy bowl of Chicken Tortilla Soup (page 97). Its creamy freshness and taste of chile are delicious.

1/2 cup reduced-calorie mayonnaise
1/3 cup plain fat-free Greek yogurt
1/4 cup fat-free sour cream
1/4 cup chopped Roasted Green Chiles (page 152)
3/4 tsp salt

1. In a food processor, pulse mayonnaise, yogurt, sour cream, chiles, and salt until smooth and well blended.
2. Serve immediately, or refrigerate in an airtight container or squeeze bottle, stirring occasionally, for up to 3 days.

Tex-Mex Chile Gravy

This saucy, thin beefy gravy is laced with red chile seasoning for authentic Tex-Mex flavor. It's typically served over cheese enchiladas, but it's also delicious over burritos with cheese melted on top, known in some places as a "saddle."

1/4 cup olive oil
1/4 cup whole-wheat flour
1 tsp black pepper
1 tsp garlic powder
1/4 tsp salt
2 tsp ground cumin
2 Tbsp chili powder
1/8 tsp cayenne
2 cups low-sodium beef broth

1. In a large skillet, heat oil over medium heat.
2. Lower heat, add flour, and stir continuously until the roux turns a light golden brown.
3. Add the black pepper, garlic powder, salt, cumin, chili powder, and cayenne, and continue to cook for 1 minute, stirring constantly.
4. Slowly add broth, stirring until the sauce thickens.
5. Turn heat to low and let sauce simmer for 10–15 minutes. Add water, 1 Tbsp at a time, to adjust to the desired thickness.

Variation: For beef Chile Gravy, in a small skillet, brown 1/4 lb ground beef and 1/2 cup water over medium heat. Crumble meat into small pieces as it cooks. Slowly add the meat to the gravy in Step 2.

Serves: 8
Serving Size: 1/4 cup
Prep Time: 10 minutes
Cook Time: 18 minutes

Choices/Exchanges

1 1/2 Fat

Basic Nutritional Values

Calories	80
Calories from Fat	60
Total Fat	7.0 g
Saturated Fat	1.0 g
Trans Fat	0.0 g
Cholesterol	0 mg
Sodium	125 mg
Potassium	100 mg
Total Carbohydrate	4 g
Dietary Fiber	1 g
Sugars	0 g
Protein	2 g
Phosphorus	30 mg

Fresh Veggie Enchilada Sauce

Serves: 8
Serving Size: 1/4 cup
Prep Time: 10 minutes
Cook Time: 13 minutes

Choices/Exchanges

1 Fat

This sauce is light, yet it has a nice spicy flavor. A Sonoran-style sauce with less chile and more gravy, it's perfect for ladling over burritos and cheese enchiladas.

2 Tbsp olive oil
3 cloves garlic, minced
1 tomato, seeded and diced
1/2 cup diced onion
2 Tbsp whole-wheat flour
1 1/2 cups reduced-sodium chicken stock (see Note)
1/2 cup chopped Roasted Green Chiles (page 152)

1. In a large skillet, heat oil over medium-low heat.
2. Add garlic, tomato, and onion, stirring until onions are soft, about 6 minutes.
3. Add flour and stir, coating onion and tomato, and cook for 1 minute more.
4. Slowly add stock and green chiles, stirring as sauce thickens, 4–6 minutes.
5. Serve immediately, or let cool completely and refrigerate for up to 2 days or freeze for up to 3 months.

Note: Depending on use, substitute reduced-sodium beef stock for chicken stock.

Basic Nutritional Values

Calories	50
Calories from Fat	30
Total Fat	3.5 g
Saturated Fat	0.5 g
Trans Fat	0.0 g
Cholesterol	0 mg
Sodium	110 mg
Potassium	160 mg
Total Carbohydrate	4 g
Dietary Fiber	1 g
Sugars	1 g
Protein	1 g
Phosphorus	30 mg

Tip

For a thinner sauce, add additional stock, 1–2 Tbsp at a time.

Red Enchilada Sauce

Red Enchilada Sauce is a rich earthy sauce that turns a corn tortilla into a meal! It makes the perfect enchilada and covers a grilled steak like no other sauce can. I make it ahead so I always have some on hand.

5 Tbsp olive oil or canola oil, divided use
4 cloves garlic, minced
2 cups Red Chile Purée (page 66) or a store-bought brand of your choice
2 Tbsp whole-wheat flour
1 tsp kosher salt

1. In a large skillet, heat 2 Tbsp of oil over medium heat.
2. Add garlic and sauté for 1–2 minutes. Add chile purée. Bring to a gentle boil. Reduce heat to low and simmer, stirring occasionally, until flavors are well blended, 8–10 minutes. Set aside.
3. In a small bowl, add remaining oil. Gradually stir in flour, creating a thick paste.
4. Gradually stir flour paste into chile sauce over medium heat. Stir in salt. Reduce heat and simmer, stirring, until thick and smooth, 6–8 minutes.
5. Serve immediately. Or cool to room temperature, then refrigerate in an airtight container for up to 2 days.

Serves: 10
Serving Size: 1/4 cup
Prep Time: 8 minutes
Cook Time: 20 minutes

Choices/Exchanges
1 Nonstarchy Vegetable,
1 1/2 Fat

Basic Nutritional Values

Calories	80
Calories from Fat	60
Total Fat	7.0 g
Saturated Fat	1.0 g
Trans Fat	0.0 g
Cholesterol	0 mg
Sodium	200 mg
Potassium	105 mg
Total Carbohydrate	5 g
Dietary Fiber	2 g
Sugars	2 g
Protein	1 g
Phosphorus	15 mg

'hile Enchilada Sauce

Serves: 8
Serving Size: 1/4 cup
Prep Time: 6 minutes
Cook Time: 20 minutes

Choices/Exchanges

1 Fat

Basic Nutritional Values

Calories	50
Calories from Fat	30
Total Fat	3.5 g
Saturated Fat	0.5 g
Trans Fat	0.0 g
Cholesterol	0 mg
Sodium	20 mg
Potassium	170 mg
Total Carbohydrate	4 g
Dietary Fiber	1 g
Sugars	1 g
Protein	1 g
Phosphorus	40 mg

The fresh flavor of roasted green chiles is the foundation of this sauce. This versatile sauce is delicious over burritos, eggs, roasted chicken, and so many Tex-Mex favorites.

1 1/2 cups chopped Roasted Green Chiles (page 152)
2 cloves garlic, minced
1 cup low-sodium chicken stock
2 Tbsp olive oil
1/4 cup whole-wheat flour

1. In a large skillet, combine chiles, garlic, and stock and bring to a boil over medium-high heat. Reduce heat and boil gently for about 6–8 minutes.
2. In a small bowl add oil. Gradually stir in flour, creating a thick paste. Stir until smooth.
3. Gradually stir paste into chile mixture in skillet over medium heat. Whisk until smooth and thick, 6–8 minutes.
4. Serve immediately. Or cool to room temperature, then refrigerate in an airtight container for up to 2 days.

Sweet Chile Sauce

This little sauce is so versatile—I add it to my Spicy Margarita (page 10), and drizzle it over Pork Carnitas Tacos (page 114) for a sweet/savory flavor.

3/4 cup sugar-free boysenberry or raspberry jam
1 tsp crushed red pepper flakes

1. In a small pot, combine jam and red pepper flakes and heat over low heat, stirring, until jam is melted and flavors are infused.
2. Strain through a fine mesh strainer into a bowl to remove seeds and flakes.
3. Let cool to room temperature. Store in an airtight container.

Serves: 12
Serving Size: 1 Tbsp
Prep Time: 4 minutes
Cook Time: 8 minutes

Choices/Exchanges

Free food

Basic Nutritional Values

Calories	10
Calories from Fat	0
Total Fat	0.0 g
Saturated Fat	0.0 g
Trans Fat	0.0 g
Cholesterol	0 mg
Sodium	0 mg
Potassium	15 mg
Total Carbohydrate	3 g
Dietary Fiber	2 g
Sugars	0 g
Protein	0 g
Phosphorus	0 mg

RED CHILE PURÉE

This is a long process, but the result gives you an authentic chile flavor. I use Red Chile Purée in my Tex-Mex Chile con Carne (page 99) and Red Enchilada Sauce (page 63).

Serves: 8
Serving Size: 1/4 cup
Prep Time: 24 hours
Process Time: 15 minutes

Choices/Exchanges

1 Nonstarchy Vegetable

6–8 dried New Mexico red chile peppers, stems removed (see Note)
Water

1. Place chiles in a bowl, fill with enough water to cover, and refrigerate overnight. This will soften the chiles.
2. Drain liquid from softened chiles, and reserve liquid for use later in this recipe.
3. In a food processor, purée chiles with 1 1/2 cups reserved liquid until smooth. Purée should be thick but pourable. Add remaining liquid, if needed.
4. Press chile purée through a fine-mesh sieve or a strainer, discarding skin and seeds.
5. Use immediately or transfer to an airtight container and refrigerate for up to 4 days or freeze up to 3 months.

Note: You can find frozen red chiles in the frozen-food section at your local grocery store.

Basic Nutritional Values	
Calories	20
Calories from Fat	0
Total Fat	0.0 g
Saturated Fat	0.1 g
Trans Fat	0.0 g
Cholesterol	0 mg
Sodium	10 mg
Potassium	120 mg
Total Carbohydrate	4 g
Dietary Fiber	2 g
Sugars	3 g
Protein	1 g
Phosphorus	10 mg

Tortillas and Breads

Tortillas have evolved throughout the years. I grew up enjoying fresh tortillas made by a friend's grandmother. Making them by hand is truly an art. It might be easier to get fresh tortillas these days from your local grocery store or a tortilla shop, but I offer a few recipes that you can create at home.

Fresh Whole-Grain Flour Tortillas (8-inch) 70

Fresh Whole-Grain Flour Tortillas (10-inch) 71

Fresh Corn Tortillas 72

Light Sopapillas 73

Sidebars:

    Baked Tostada Shells 74

    Reheating Tortillas 75

Whole-Grain Flour Tortillas (8-inch)

Serves: 12
Serving Size: 1 tortilla (approximately 8 inches in diameter)
Prep Time: 15 minutes
Cook Time: 12 minutes

Choices/Exchanges
1 1/2 Starch, 1/2 Fat

Basic Nutritional Values

Calories	150
Calories from Fat	45
Total Fat	5.0 g
Saturated Fat	0.4 g
Trans Fat	0.0 g
Cholesterol	0 mg
Sodium	240 mg
Potassium	90 mg
Total Carbohydrate	22 g
Dietary Fiber	3 g
Sugars	0 g
Protein	4 g
Phosphorus	80 mg

These tortillas are so good right out of the pan!

1 cup all-purpose flour
2 cups whole-wheat flour
1 1/4 tsp salt
1/4 cup vegetable oil
1 1/4 cups very warm (almost hot) water
13 sheets wax paper, cut into 10-inch squares

1. In a large bowl, combine flours and salt. Using your fingers, slowly work the oil into the flour mixture. Add small amounts of water and continue to work with hands until dough is smooth. Form a large ball. Turn out onto a floured surface. Knead the dough thoroughly.
2. Divide dough into 12 small balls. Sprinkle each ball with additional flour, and place in an airtight container for at least 15–18 minutes or for up to 1 hour.
3. On a lightly floured work surface, use a rolling pin to roll each ball into a circle, approximately 8 inches in diameter. To ensure that you get a round tortilla, turn your dough one-quarter turn each time you roll it.
4. Transfer rolled tortilla to a wax-paper square. Repeat with each dough ball. Stack uncooked tortillas on a platter.
5. Heat a dry nonstick or cast-iron skillet over medium heat. One tortilla at a time, remove wax paper and transfer tortilla to skillet. Cook, turning once, for about 30 to 40 seconds per side or until bubbling and lightly browned.
6. Transfer tortilla to a towel-lined plate. Repeat Step 5 with next tortilla. Wrap in towel to keep warm.
7. Serve immediately.

For later use: Cooked tortillas can be stored in an airtight container and kept in the refrigerator for up to 3 days or frozen for up to about 2 months.

Fresh Whole-Grain Flour Tortillas (10-inch)

3 cups whole-wheat flour
1/2 tsp salt
1/4 cup canola oil
1 1/4 cups very warm (almost hot) water
9 sheets wax paper, cut into 10-inch squares

1. In a large bowl, combine flour and salt. Using your fingers, slowly work the oil into the flour mixture. Add small amounts of water and continue to work with hands until dough is smooth. Form a large ball. Turn out onto a floured surface. Knead the dough thoroughly.
2. Divide dough into 8 balls. Sprinkle each ball with additional flour, and place in an airtight container. Cover and let dough stand for at least 15–18 minutes or for up to 1 hour.
3. On a lightly floured work surface, use a rolling pin rubbed with flour to roll each ball into a circle, 10 inches in diameter. To ensure that you get a round tortilla, turn your dough one-quarter turn each time you roll it.
4. Transfer rolled tortilla to a wax-paper square. Repeat with each dough ball. Stack uncooked tortillas on a platter.
5. Heat a dry nonstick or cast-iron skillet over medium heat. One tortilla at a time, remove wax paper and transfer tortilla to skillet. Cook, turning once, for about 45 seconds per side or until bubbling and lightly browned.
6. Transfer tortilla to a towel-lined plate. Repeat Step 5 with next tortilla. Wrap in towel to keep warm.
7. Serve immediately.

For later use: Cooked tortillas can be stored in an airtight container and kept in the refrigerator for up to 3 days or frozen for up to about 2 months.

Serves: 8
Serving Size: 1 tortilla
  (approximately 10 inches in diameter)
Prep Time: About 20 minutes
Cook Time: 12 minutes

Choices/Exchanges

2 Starch, 1 Fat

Basic Nutritional Values

Calories	210
Calories from Fat	70
Total Fat	8.0 g
Saturated Fat	0.6 g
Trans Fat	0.0 g
Cholesterol	0 mg
Sodium	150 mg
Potassium	180 mg
Total Carbohydrate	33 g
Dietary Fiber	5 g
Sugars	0 g
Protein	6 g
Phosphorus	155 mg

Fresh Corn Tortillas

Serves: 16
Serving Size: 1 tortilla
(6 inches in diameter)
Prep Time: 15 minutes
Cook Time: 16 minutes

Choices/Exchanges

1 Starch

Basic Nutritional Values

Calories	60
Calories from Fat	5
Total Fat	0.5 g
Saturated Fat	0.1 g
Trans Fat	0.0 g
Cholesterol	0 mg
Sodium	95 mg
Potassium	45 mg
Total Carbohydrate	12 g
Dietary Fiber	2 g
Sugars	0 g
Protein	1 g
Phosphorus	35 mg

Fresh corn tortillas are a simple, authentic bread. Preparing them takes a little work, but the result will melt in your mouth.

2 cups masa harina
1/2 tsp salt
1/4 tsp baking soda
1 1/2 cups very warm (almost hot) water
17 sheets wax paper, cut into 10-inch squares
Tortilla press

1. In a large bowl, mix together masa harina, salt, baking soda, and water. Knead with your hands to form the masa dough.
2. Divide dough into 16 small balls. Place balls in an airtight container as you make each one (for up to 1 hour).
3. To press tortillas, place a piece of wax paper in tortilla press and place masa ball on top. Place another piece of wax paper on top of dough and press to a 6-inch circle. Continue with remaining balls, stacking uncooked tortillas on a plate with a sheet of wax paper between each one.
4. Heat a dry nonstick or cast-iron skillet over medium heat. One tortilla at a time, remove wax paper and transfer tortilla to skillet. Cook, turning once, for about 30 to 40 seconds per side or until bubbling and lightly browned.
5. Transfer tortilla to a towel-lined plate. Wrap in towel to keep warm. Repeat Step 4 with next tortilla ball. Serve immediately.

Light Sopapillas

These little pastry puffs can be a savory treat or a sweet treat. Stove-top cooking instead of frying makes them a much healthier option. Dust them with powdered sugar and serve with honey for a sweet dish, or stuff them with a taco filling and fresh garnish for a savory dish.

1 cup all-purpose flour
1 cup whole-wheat flour
2 tsp baking powder
1 Tbsp shortening
1/2 tsp salt
1 1/2 cup warm water
Cooking spray

1. In a large bowl, combine flours, baking powder, shortening, and salt. Using an electric stand mixer with paddle attachment mixer on low speed, gradually beat in the warm water. Mix for 2–3 minutes.
2. Continue to mix until dough is stiff and not sticky to the touch. Cover and let stand for 30 minutes.
3. Place half of the dough onto a lightly floured surface. Roll out to 1/8-inch thickness. With a knife, cut into 2-inch squares. Once rolled out, roll each square out one more time, as thin as paper.
4. Heat a large, heavy skillet over high heat. Spray the skillet liberally with cooking spray.
5. Place the dough in the hot skillet. As the dough puffs up, turn it gently and cook until golden brown and puffy, about 2–3 minutes. Repeat with remaining dough. Cook until all pieces are puffed up and golden brown. Spray the tops of the breads with cooking spray and flip them over. Cook an additional 2–3 minutes. Serve warm.

Serves: 14
Serving Size: 1 puff
Prep Time: 40 minutes
Cook Time: 1 hour

Choices/Exchanges

1 Starch

Basic Nutritional Values

Calories	70
Calories from Fat	10
Total Fat	1.0 g
Saturated Fat	0.3 g
Trans Fat	0.0 g
Cholesterol	0 mg
Sodium	135 mg
Potassium	45 mg
Total Carbohydrate	13 g
Dietary Fiber	1 g
Sugars	0 g
Protein	2 g
Phosphorus	105 mg

BAKED TOSTADA SHELLS

Light, crispy shells make the best tostadas. Baked shells are quick and easy to make.

8 (6-inch) Fresh Corn Tortillas (page 72)
Cooking spray

1. Preheat oven to 400°F.
2. Spray both sides of each tortilla lightly with cooking spray.
3. Place tortillas on a baking sheet and bake, turning once, until crispy and lightly browned, 4–6 minutes per side.

Serves: 8
Serving Size: 1 corn tostada (6 inches in diameter)
Prep Time: 6 minutes
Cook Time: 12 minutes

Choices/Exchanges

1 Starch

Basic Nutritional Values

Calories	60
Calories from Fat	10
Total Fat	1.0 g
Saturated Fat	0.2 g
Trans Fat	0.0 g
Cholesterol	0 mg
Sodium	95 mg
Potassium	45 mg
Total Carbohydrate	12 g
Dietary Fiber	2 g
Sugars	0 g
Protein	1 g
Phosphorus	35 mg

REHEATING TORTILLAS

I typically have to reheat the tortillas for my Tex-Mex recipes, even when the tortillas are made from scratch. Even the freshest tortillas from your local grocery store need to be reheated so that they're soft, pliable, and easy to work with. Heating tortillas is an essential element in the success of my recipes. Corn tortillas need a bit more moisture in the reheating process than flour tortillas do. Here I offer different methods for each.

Reheating Crispy, Folded Taco Shells

1. Preheat oven to 200°F.
2. Place taco shells on a baking sheet, pop them in the oven, and heat them for 8–10 minutes.

Skillet-Warmed Corn or Flour Tortillas

1. Heat a dry nonstick or cast-iron skillet over medium heat.
2. Place a tortilla in the skillet and heat each side by turning once until warm and pliable, about 1 minute per side.
3. Place in a tortilla warmer or wrap in foil to keep warm until ready to use.

Micro-Warmed Corn or Flour Tortillas

This method gives you very pliable and soft tortillas and allows you to roll them tightly, so it's perfect for preparing rolled tacos, taquitos, and enchiladas. It is also quick and easy for soft tacos.

> **Tip**
> For a moister consistency, spray each side of a corn tortilla with water.

1. Place 3–4 tortillas in a small plastic storage bag, and close or fold over the opening.
2. Microwave on High for 25–30 seconds (depending on the power of your microwave).
3. Remove the tortillas from the plastic bag. They should be warm and pliable.
4. Place in a tortilla warmer or wrap in foil to keep warm until ready to use, no longer than 5–10 minutes.

Breakfast Favorites

Starting your day with an authentic Tex-Mex breakfast gets you ahead of the rest! Enjoy quesadillas and tacos, filled with delicate eggs, chiles, and cheese—Tex-Mex breakfasts rock!

Breakfast Quesadilla 79

Tex-Mex Breakfast Tacos 80

Huevos Rancheros 81

Chorizo, Potato, and Egg Burrito—Smothered 82

Chilaquiles with Eggs 83

Chile Papas 84

Pan Huevos with Avocado 85

Spiced Fresh Fruit and Yogurt Parfait 86

Whole-Wheat Morning Toast with Cajeta and Coconut 87

Mexican Bread Pudding with Fresh Berries 89

Breakfast Quesadilla

Fluffy eggs and spicy chiles folded into a tortilla with rich melted cheese makes breakfast a pleasure! Lightly toasted to perfection, this quesadilla redefines breakfast.

Cooking spray
1/4 cup chopped Roasted Green Chiles (page 152)
4 eggs, beaten
1/4 tsp pepper
2 (10-inch) Fresh Whole-Grain Flour Tortillas (page 71)
1 1/2 cups shredded reduced-fat cheddar cheese (see Note)
4 strips turkey bacon, cooked crisp and crumbled

1. Coat a small skillet lightly with cooking spray.
2. Sauté green chiles over medium-low heat for 1–2 minutes. Add beaten eggs and cook, stirring, until scrambled and set. Season with pepper.
3. Coat a second, large skillet lightly with cooking spray. Place one tortilla in the skillet, and cook over medium heat until air bubbles begin to form, about 1 minute. Flip tortilla over and cook for 1 minute more (do not let tortilla get crispy).
4. Spread half the cheese evenly over the tortilla, covering to the edges.
5. Reduce heat to low. Quickly arrange half the cooked bacon and half the egg mixture over the cheese. Cook until the cheese starts to melt, about 1 minute.
6. Fold tortilla in half to create a half-moon shape. Flip folded tortilla over, and cook until it is lightly toasted and the cheese filling is completely melted, 1–2 minutes.
7. Transfer quesadilla to a cutting board. Recoat the skillet with cooking spray, and repeat with second tortilla and remaining cheese, bacon, and egg mixture.
8. Cut each quesadilla into 3 wedges and serve immediately with a fresh salsa.

Note: I use a variety of cheeses, such as asadero, Monterey Jack, and white cheddar. Find your favorite.

Variation: For chorizo quesadillas, substitute 4 oz cooked beef or pork chorizo (drained) for the bacon. Follow Step 5.

Serves: 6
Serving Size: 1 wedge
Prep Time: 15 minutes
Cook Time: 16 minutes

Choices/Exchanges

1/2 Starch,
2 Medium-Fat Protein

Basic Nutritional Values

Calories	160
Calories from Fat	90
Total Fat	10.0 g
Saturated Fat	4.2 g
Trans Fat	0.0 g
Cholesterol	140 mg
Sodium	460 mg
Potassium	135 mg
Total Carbohydrate	8 g
Dietary Fiber	5 g
Sugars	1 g
Protein	14 g
Phosphorus	260 mg

Tex-Mex Breakfast Tacos

These breakfast tacos are a Tex-Mex favorite! The chorizo—a spicy Mexican sausage—and eggs are perfect together, nestled in a warm Fresh Corn Tortilla (page 72).

Serves: 8
Serving Size: 1 taco
Prep Time: 10 minutes
Cook Time: 12 minutes

Choices/Exchanges

1 Starch, 1 Medium-Fat Protein

Cooking spray
4 oz fresh chorizo, removed from casings
4 eggs, lightly beaten
8 (6-inch) Fresh Corn Tortillas (page 72), skillet-warmed (page 75)
1 cup shredded reduced-fat cheddar or Monterey Jack cheese

1. Spray a medium-sized skillet with cooking spray, add chorizo, and cook over medium-low heat, breaking up with a spoon until well browned, 8–10 minutes. Drain excess grease.
2. Add eggs, and cook, stirring, until set.
3. To build the tacos, divide egg mixture equally among tortillas. Top with cheese. Fold tortillas in half. Serve immediately.

Variation: For a double meat flavor, add 2 strips turkey bacon, cooked crisp and crumbled in Step 1.

Basic Nutritional Values

Calories	140
Calories from Fat	60
Total Fat	7.0 g
Saturated Fat	3.0 g
Trans Fat	0.1 g
Cholesterol	105 mg
Sodium	320 mg
Potassium	120 mg
Total Carbohydrate	12 g
Dietary Fiber	2 g
Sugars	0 g
Protein	9 g
Phosphorus	160 mg

Tip

This breakfast taco takes very little time to prepare, and all 8 tacos can be made ahead and kept warm, covered, for up to 1 hour in an oven preheated to 200°F. If you're on the go, wrap each taco individually in foil to take with you.

Huevos Rancheros

There are many versions of this well-known breakfast plate. Tex-Mex Huevos Rancheros calls for a fresh salsa ladled over eggs and Fresh Corn Tortillas (page 72).

1 cup Tex-Mex Salsa (page 49) or a store-bought brand of your choice (see Note)
4 (6-inch) Fresh Corn Tortillas (page 72)
4 eggs
1/2 cup shredded reduced-fat cheddar cheese

1. In a small saucepan, warm the salsa. Keep on low heat, stirring occasionally.
2. Lightly spray both sides of each tortilla with cooking spray. In a large skillet over high heat, warm tortillas on both sides until they are pliable and heated through. Set aside.
3. Recoat the skillet with cooking spray. Break the eggs into the skillet and fry each egg, turning once for "over medium," 1–2 minutes per side, or to desired doneness.
4. Working quickly, place each tortilla on an individual ovenproof plate and place 1 egg on top of each tortilla. Top eggs equally with warmed salsa, then with cheese. Broil until cheese is melted, about 1 minute. Serve immediately.

Note: For a saucier ranchero style, substitute 1 cup Red Enchilada Sauce (page 63) or Green Chile Enchilada Sauce (page 64) for the salsa.

Serves: 4
Serving Size: 1 huevos rancheros
Prep Time: 8 minutes
Cook Time: 4 minutes

Choices/Exchanges

1 Starch,
1 Medium-Fat Protein,
1/2 Fat

Basic Nutritional Values

Calories	170
Calories from Fat	70
Total Fat	8.0 g
Saturated Fat	3.0 g
Trans Fat	0.0 g
Cholesterol	190 mg
Sodium	340 mg
Potassium	270 mg
Total Carbohydrate	16 g
Dietary Fiber	2 g
Sugars	2 g
Protein	11 g
Phosphorus	210 mg

Chorizo, Potato, and Egg Burrito—Smothered

Serves: 4
Serving Size: 1 burrito
Prep Time: 10 minutes
Cook Time: About 45 minutes

Choices/Exchanges

3 Starch, 2 Nonstarchy Vegetable, 1 Medium-Fat Protein, 3 1/2 Fat

Basic Nutritional Values

Calories	510
Calories from Fat	220
Total Fat	25.0 g
Saturated Fat	6.1 g
Trans Fat	0.1 g
Cholesterol	205 mg
Sodium	560 mg
Potassium	980 mg
Total Carbohydrate	52 g
Dietary Fiber	9 g
Sugars	4 g
Protein	22 g
Phosphorus	480 mg

This hearty breakfast burrito will fill a plate and keep you full all day! I like the rich flavor of chorizo, but you can use other meats, such as pork sausage, ground beef, or bacon.

Cooking spray
4 oz chorizo
1 potato, cut into 1/4-inch dice
4 eggs, lightly beaten
4 (10-inch) Fresh Whole-Grain Flour Tortillas (page 71), skillet-warmed (page 75)
1/2 cup shredded reduced-fat cheddar cheese, divided use
2 cups Green Enchilada Sauce (page 64) or Red Enchilada Sauce (page 63)
2 cups shredded lettuce
1 cup diced tomatoes

1. Preheat oven to 400°F.
2. Spray a medium-sized skillet with cooking spray. Add chorizo and cook over medium-low heat, breaking up with a spoon until well browned, 8–10 minutes. Drain excess grease. Transfer to a bowl and set aside.
3. Wipe skillet with a paper towel. Recoat the skillet with cooking spray. Add potato and cook, covered, stirring occasionally, until potato is soft, 10–12 minutes. Remove lid and cook, stirring, until potato is lightly browned and crispy, 8–10 minutes more. Transfer to a bowl and set aside.
4. Reduce heat to medium-low. Recoat the skillet with cooking spray. Add eggs and cook, stirring, until set. Return chorizo and potato to skillet, and mix well until heated through.
5. To build the burritos, divide egg mixture equally in center of each tortilla. Divide 1/4 cup cheese among the burritos. Fold bottom edge of tortilla up over filling. Starting at folded bottom edge, roll up to enclose filling. Secure with a toothpick.
6. Place each burrito on an individual ovenproof plate. Spoon sauce on top, dividing equally, and sprinkle burritos with remaining cheese. Bake until cheese is melted and bubbly and burrito is heated through, 8–10 minutes. Garnish each with equal amounts of lettuce and tomato.

Tip

If you're on the go, make hand-held burritos by omitting the sauce and cheese from Step 6.

Chilaquiles with Eggs

In this dish (pronounced *chill-ah-kee-les*), crunchy corn tortilla chips are simmered in a warm chile sauce and topped with cheese and eggs. Instead of lightly fried corn tortilla strips, I cut calories and reduce fat by using baked corn tortilla chips.

24 Baked Crispy Corn Tortilla Chips (page 20) or a store-bought brand of your choice

1 cup Tex-Mex Salsa (page 49) or store-bought tomato-based salsa in a brand of your choice

1 cup Roasted Tomatillo Chile Sauce (page 50) or store-bought green chile–based salsa in a brand of your choice

3/4 cup shredded reduced-fat cheddar cheese

4 eggs

2 green onions, mostly green part, minced

2 Tbsp minced cilantro

1 avocado, seeded, peeled, and thinly sliced

1. Place chips in a large skillet coated with cooking spray over medium heat. Slowly add salsa and chile sauce. Top with cheddar cheese. Reduce heat, and simmer until chips are soft yet still crispy on some edges, about 6–8 minutes.
2. While tortilla chips are simmering, coat a small skillet with cooking spray and fry eggs, turning once for "over medium," 1–2 minutes per side. Place fried eggs side by side on top of chips.
3. To serve, scoop servings of chips and egg onto individual plates. Garnish with onions, cilantro, and avocado slices.

Serves: 4
Serving Size: About 6 topped chips with 1 egg
Prep Time: 8 minutes
Cook Time: 12 minutes

Choices/Exchanges

1 Starch, 2 Nonstarchy Vegetable, 1 Lean Protein, 2 1/2 Fat

Basic Nutritional Values

Calories	280
Calories from Fat	140
Total Fat	15.0 g
Saturated Fat	4.6 g
Trans Fat	0.0 g
Cholesterol	195 mg
Sodium	470 mg
Potassium	670 mg
Total Carbohydrate	24 g
Dietary Fiber	6 g
Sugars	5 g
Protein	14 g
Phosphorus	295 mg

Chile Papas

Serves: 6
Serving Size: About 3/4 cup
Prep Time: 18 minutes
Cook Time: 45 minutes

Choices/Exchanges

1 Starch, 1/2 Carbohydrate,
1 Medium-Fat Protein

Basic Nutritional Values

Calories	180
Calories from Fat	60
Total Fat	7.0 g
Saturated Fat	2.7 g
Trans Fat	0.0 g
Cholesterol	20 mg
Sodium	470 mg
Potassium	600 mg
Total Carbohydrate	23 g
Dietary Fiber	3 g
Sugars	3 g
Protein	8 g
Phosphorus	190 mg

This hearty potato creation is such a good dish for people who don't eat eggs. I like to serve it for breakfast, but it also makes a welcome side for lunch or dinner.

1 Tbsp olive oil
4 medium baking potatoes (unpeeled), cut into 1-inch pieces
3/4 tsp seasoned salt
1 cup chopped Roasted Green Chiles (page 152)
4 slices turkey bacon, cooked and crumbled
3/4 cup shredded reduced-fat Monterey Jack cheese
3/4 cup fat-free sour cream

1. Preheat oven to 375°F.
2. In a large skillet, heat oil over medium-high heat. Add potatoes and cook, covered, until tender, 10–15 minutes, stirring occasionally. Remove lid, season with salt, and cook until golden brown and crispy, 8–10 minutes.
3. Place potatoes on ovenproof serving platter. Top evenly with layers of chiles, bacon, and cheese. Bake until potatoes are heated through and cheese is melted, 18–20 minutes.
4. To serve, spoon potatoes onto individual plates and garnish with sour cream.

Pan Huevos with Avocado

Tex-Mex toast is full of flavor—avocado, egg—and freshness! A great way to start the day!

Butter-flavored cooking spray
4 thin slices (3/4 oz each) whole-wheat bread (such as Sara Lee Delightful)
2 medium avocados, seeded, peeled, and mashed
4 eggs
4 Tbsp Pico de Gallo (page 48) or store-bought salsa in a brand of your choice

1. Coat a medium-sized skillet lightly with cooking spray. Place 2 pieces of bread in the skillet, and cook over medium-high heat until lightly toasted. Repeat with remaining slices of bread.
2. Spread each piece of toast evenly with mashed avocado, and place on individual serving plates.
3. Recoat the skillet lightly with cooking spray. Fry each egg, turning once for "over medium," 1–2 minutes per side. Place each egg on top of avocado toast. Garnish evenly with salsa.

Note: The eggs can be scrambled instead of fried. When scrambled eggs have finished cooking, divide evenly on slices of avocado toast.

Serves: 4
Serving Size: 1 open-faced sandwich
Prep Time: 12 minutes
Cook Time: 8 minutes

Choices/Exchanges

1/2 Starch, 1/2 Fruit, 1 Lean Protein, 3 Fat

Basic Nutritional Values

Calories	240
Calories from Fat	140
Total Fat	16.0 g
Saturated Fat	3.3 g
Trans Fat	0.0 g
Cholesterol	185 mg
Sodium	190 mg
Potassium	560 mg
Total Carbohydrate	17 g
Dietary Fiber	8 g
Sugars	3 g
Protein	11 g
Phosphorus	195 mg

Spiced Fresh Fruit and Yogurt Parfait

Serves: 4
Serving Size: 1/2 cup yogurt and 1 cup fruit
Prep Time: 12 minutes
Chill Time: 30 minutes

Choices/Exchanges
1 1/2 Fruit, 1/2 Fat-Free Milk

Basic Nutritional Values

Calories	140
Calories from Fat	10
Total Fat	1.0 g
Saturated Fat	0.1 g
Trans Fat	0.0 g
Cholesterol	10 mg
Sodium	40 mg
Potassium	440 mg
Total Carbohydrate	27 g
Dietary Fiber	4 g
Sugars	18 g
Protein	11 g
Phosphorus	155 mg

Fresh fruit spiked with a hint of chile and citrus wakes up the taste buds! The fruit-yogurt combination is so refreshing.

3 kiwis, peeled and cut into bite-size pieces
1 pint strawberries, stemmed and chopped
1 cup blueberries
2 Tbsp orange juice
1 tsp crushed red pepper flakes
2 cups fat-free reduced-sugar vanilla-flavored Greek yogurt

1. In a large bowl, gently combine kiwis, strawberries, and blueberries. Add orange juice and crushed red pepper flakes. Toss together until all fruit is well coated. Cover and refrigerate until chilled, stirring occasionally, for 30 minutes or up to 2 hours.
2. Place 1/2 cup yogurt in each individual serving bowl or stemmed glassware. Top with fruit mixture and serve.

Whole-Wheat Morning Toast with Cajeta and Coconut

This sweet bread entrée—rich in caramel flavor but low in calories—is perfect for a special morning celebration.

4 eggs
2 egg whites
8 thin slices (3/4 oz each) whole-wheat bread (such as Sara Lee Delightful)
1 Tbsp butter
1/3 cup low-calorie brown sugar blend (such as Splenda)
2 Tbsp almond milk
2 Tbsp shredded unsweetened coconut

1. Preheat oven to 200°F.
2. In a medium-sized bowl, whip eggs and egg whites until well blended.
3. Coat a large skillet lightly with cooking spray, and heat to medium. Dip each slice of bread into egg mixture, and place in skillet. Cook each piece of toast for 1–2 minutes on each side. Repeat. Place on a serving platter and keep warm in oven.
4. For the cajeta (pronounced *kah-heh-tah*) sauce, in a small saucepan, melt butter and low-calorie brown sugar blend together over medium-low heat until mixture bubbles. Add almond milk and whisk until smooth, about 1 minute. Remove from heat.
5. Place two slices of toast on an individual serving plate. Drizzle evenly with cajeta sauce and sprinkle with coconut. Repeat with remaining toast, sauce, and coconut.

Serves: 4
Serving Size: 2 slices
Prep Time: 6 minutes
Cook Time: 18 minutes

Choices/Exchanges

1 Starch, 1 Carbohydrate, 1 Medium-Fat Protein, 1 Fat

Basic Nutritional Values

Calories	270
Calories from Fat	90
Total Fat	10.0 g
Saturated Fat	5.0 g
Trans Fat	0.1 g
Cholesterol	195 mg
Sodium	320 mg
Potassium	250 mg
Total Carbohydrate	34 g
Dietary Fiber	5 g
Sugars	10 g
Protein	14 g
Phosphorus	205 mg

Mexican Bread Pudding with Fresh Berries

This sweet breakfast bread has a rich custard texture and taste. Topped with fresh berries and a dusting of powdered sugar, it is a delight.

8 thin slices (3/4 oz each) whole-wheat bread (such as Sara Lee Delightful), torn into bite-size pieces
6 eggs, beaten
2 egg whites, beaten
2 cups fat-free half-and-half
1 cup zero-calorie granulated sweetener (such as Splenda)
1 tsp cinnamon
2 tsp vanilla extract
1 Tbsp powdered sugar
1 pint fresh blueberries
1 pint fresh raspberries

1. Preheat oven to 350°F.
2. Lightly coat 13 x 9-inch glass baking dish with cooking spray and fill with torn bread pieces.
3. In medium-sized mixing bowl, combine eggs, half-and-half, zero-calorie granulated sweetener, cinnamon, and vanilla extract. Mix well and pour over bread.
4. Bake for 40–45 minutes until filling is set. Bread will puff up and then settle while cooling. Cut into rectangle pieces (4 1/2 x 3 1/4 inches) and place on individual plates. Dust each piece lightly with powdered sugar. Spoon berries across plates and serve.

Serves: 8
Serving Size: 1 rectangle piece plus 1/2 cup berries
Prep Time: 12 minutes
Cook Time: 45 minutes

Choices/Exchanges

1/2 Starch, 1/2 Fruit, 1/2 Fat-Free Milk, 1/2 Carbohydrate, 1 Medium-Fat Protein

Basic Nutritional Values

Calories	190
Calories from Fat	45
Total Fat	5.0 g
Saturated Fat	1.7 g
Trans Fat	0.0 g
Cholesterol	140 mg
Sodium	220 mg
Potassium	320 mg
Total Carbohydrate	28 g
Dietary Fiber	6 g
Sugars	13 g
Protein	11 g
Phosphorus	225 mg

Soups and Stews

Steamy pots of goodness rich in spices, vegetables, poultry, and hearty meats are among the best of Tex-Mex cooking. These versions of traditional creamy chowders, savory meat medleys, and brothy favorites are light and healthier for you. Vegetable-packed soups, rich stews, and good old Tex-Mex Chile con Carne are classics you will enjoy!

Green Chile Corn Chowder 93

Albondigas 95

Red Chile Posole 96

Chicken Tortilla Soup 97

Green Chile Stew. 98

Tex-Mex Chile con Carne 99

Green Chile Corn Chowder

Chowder is my comfort food. This creamy blend is packed full of corn, zucchini, and squash, accented with a hint of chile. Reduced-fat cheeses and cream create a healthier chowder.

2 Tbsp olive oil
3 cloves garlic, minced
4 cups frozen corn kernels
2 large zucchini, chopped into 1/4-inch pieces
1 cup chopped Roasted Green Chiles (page 152)
2 cans (10.75 oz each) reduced-calorie, reduced-sodium condensed cheese soup
1 can (use soup can) water
2 1/2 cups fat-free half-and-half
1 cup shredded reduced-fat cheddar cheese

1. In a large skillet, heat oil and add garlic, corn, zucchini, and chiles. Sauté over medium heat, stirring often, until zucchini starts to soften, 10–12 minutes. Set aside.
2. In a large pot, combine condensed soup, water, and half-and-half. Simmer, stirring occasionally, for 8–10 minutes.
3. Add corn mixture to chowder. Simmer, stirring, until heated through, 10–12 minutes.
4. To serve, ladle into individual bowls and garnish with cheese.

Variation: If you have trouble finding condensed cheese soup, substitute 8 oz processed cheese spread (such as Velveeta), cubed, and an additional 1 cup fat-free half-and-half.

Serves: 8
Serving Size: 1 1/2 cups
Prep Time: 20 minutes
Cook Time: 28 minutes

Choices/Exchanges

1 Starch, 1/2 Fat-Free Milk, 1/2 Carbohydrate, 1 Nonstarchy Vegetable, 1 Fat

Basic Nutritional Values

Calories	230
Calories from Fat	80
Total Fat	9.0 g
Saturated Fat	3.2 g
Trans Fat	0.0 g
Cholesterol	15 mg
Sodium	460 mg
Potassium	970 mg
Total Carbohydrate	32 g
Dietary Fiber	3 g
Sugars	9 g
Protein	9 g
Phosphorus	310 mg

Albondigas

This is my go-to Mexican vegetable soup. I start with a simple beefy tomato broth. The meatballs add another layer of flavor, then I add more veggies and garnish. Delicious!

1 lb ground sirloin or reduced-fat ground beef
2 Tbsp long-grain white rice
1 large egg
1/4 cup fresh oregano leaves
1 3/4 tsp salt or salt substitute
1 tsp freshly ground black pepper
1 tsp olive oil
1 cup diced onion
1 cup cored, seeded, and diced red bell pepper
4 cloves garlic, minced
8 cups low-sodium beef broth
2 Tbsp tomato paste
1/2 cup chopped zucchini
2 Tbsp minced cilantro

1. In a large bowl, combine meat, rice, and egg. Mix in oregano, salt, and pepper. Roll into 1-inch balls. Cover and set aside.
2. In a large pot, heat oil over medium-low heat. Add onion and bell pepper, and cook, stirring, until softened, 3–5 minutes. Add garlic and cook, stirring, for 2 minutes.
3. Increase heat to medium-high, add broth and tomato paste, and bring to a boil.
4. Reduce heat to a simmer, add zucchini, and cook until zucchini is soft, 10–12 minutes.
5. Gently add meatballs to simmering broth. Cover, reduce heat to low, and simmer until meatballs are no longer pink inside and rice is tender, about 30 minutes.
6. Ladle soup and meatballs into individual bowls. Garnish with cilantro.

Variation: At Step 4, add 1 potato, cut into bite-size pieces, with the zucchini.

Serves: 8
Serving Size: 1 1/4 cups
Prep Time: 20 minutes
Cook Time: About 1 hour

Choices/Exchanges

1 Nonstarchy Vegetable,
3 Lean Protein

Basic Nutritional Values

Calories	160
Calories from Fat	45
Total Fat	5.0 g
Saturated Fat	1.6 g
Trans Fat	0.1 g
Cholesterol	130 mg
Sodium	450 mg
Potassium	540 mg
Total Carbohydrate	7 g
Dietary Fiber	1 g
Sugars	2 g
Protein	20 g
Phosphorus	230 mg

Red Chile Posole

Serves: 10
Serving Size: 1 cup
Prep Time: 30 minutes
Cook Time: 1 1/4 hours

Choices/Exchanges

1/2 Starch, 1 Nonstarchy Vegetable, 2 Lean Protein, 1 Fat

Basic Nutritional Values

Calories	200
Calories from Fat	90
Total Fat	10.0 g
Saturated Fat	2.9 g
Trans Fat	0.0 g
Cholesterol	40 mg
Sodium	420 mg
Potassium	350 mg
Total Carbohydrate	10 g
Dietary Fiber	2 g
Sugars	2 g
Protein	17 g
Phosphorus	130 mg

Posole is a regional favorite, typically served around the winter holidays, that celebrates life's blessings. It is a unique combination of hearty pork, hominy, and spicy red chile. The garnish—fresh lime, radishes, and green onions—elevates these flavors.

2 lb boneless (visible fat removed) pork shoulder blade (butt) roast, cubed
2 cups canned white hominy, drained and rinsed
1 tsp salt
4 cloves garlic, minced
1 Tbsp chopped dried Mexican oregano (see Note)
1 1/2 tsp ground cumin
1 1/2 cups Red Enchilada Sauce (page 63) or a store-bought brand of your choice
2 1/2 cups water
5 green onions, green part only, chopped
5–7 radishes, sliced
1/2 cup minced cilantro
2 limes, quartered

1. Place pork chunks in a large pot, and add enough water to just cover pork. Bring to a boil over medium-high heat. Cook uncovered, stirring occasionally, until pork is evenly browned and water and juices have evaporated, about 45 minutes to 1 hour. Remove from heat.
2. Stir in hominy, salt, garlic, oregano, cumin, and sauce, mixing well.
3. Slowly stir in water. Return to heat, and simmer, stirring occasionally, until completely heated through, 10–12 minutes.
4. Ladle into individual bowls and garnish with green onions, radishes, cilantro, and a wedge of lime.

Note: Usually, you can buy dried Mexican oregano in the international food section of your local grocery store. If it's not available, substitute 1 1/2 tsp regular dried oregano.

Chicken Tortilla Soup

This family favorite is perfect for a lazy weekend—or to fix and have ready before a busy week. There are many ways to customize this soup to satisfy your taste buds.

1/2 tsp ground cumin
1/2 tsp chili powder
1/2 tsp garlic powder
2 boneless, skinless chicken breasts (about 10 oz total)
2 Tbsp olive oil, divided use
1 large onion, chopped
2 cloves garlic, minced
6 cups low-sodium chicken stock
1 Tbsp tomato paste
2 cups broken Baked Crispy Corn Tortilla Chips (page 20)
2 cups shredded reduced-fat Monterey Jack or cheddar cheese
1 Tbsp crushed red pepper flakes, or to taste
4 green onions, green part only, minced
2 medium tomatoes, seeded and diced
2 Tbsp minced cilantro
3/4 cup fat-free sour cream or plain fat-free yogurt

1. In a small bowl, combine cumin, chili powder, and garlic powder. Cut each chicken breast horizontally into 2 thin slices. Rub chicken pieces with 1 Tbsp olive oil. Season each piece with cumin mixture.
2. Pan-fry chicken over medium-high heat, turning once, until golden brown and no longer pink inside, 8–10 minutes. Shred chicken, or cut it into bite-size pieces, and set aside.
3. In a large pot, combine remaining oil, onion, and garlic over medium-low heat. Stirring occasionally, cook until onion is transparent, 8–10 minutes.
4. Add stock, tomato paste, and chicken. Reduce heat to low. Cover and simmer for 15 minutes.
5. To serve, divide chips equally in soup bowls and ladle soup over chips. Top with cheese. Garnish each bowl with a pinch of red pepper flakes, green onions, tomatoes, and cilantro. Top each bowl with a dollop of sour cream.

Variation: For a creamier version, add 1/2 cup fat-free sour cream at Step 4 and blend well.

Serves: 8
Serving Size: 1 cup
Prep Time: 20 minutes
Cook Time: 35 minutes

Choices/Exchanges

1/2 Carbohydrate,
1 Nonstarchy Vegetable,
3 Lean Protein, 1 Fat

Basic Nutritional Values

Calories	240
Calories from Fat	100
Total Fat	11.0 g
Saturated Fat	4.4 g
Trans Fat	0.0 g
Cholesterol	45 mg
Sodium	450 mg
Potassium	480 mg
Total Carbohydrate	16 g
Dietary Fiber	2 g
Sugars	4 g
Protein	22 g
Phosphorus	300 mg

Green Chile Stew

Serves: 8
Serving Size: 1 cup
Prep Time: 20 minutes
Cook Time: About 2 1/2 hours

Choices/Exchanges

2 Nonstarchy Vegetable,
3 Lean Protein, 1 1/2 Fat

Basic Nutritional Values

Calories	250
Calories from Fat	110
Total Fat	12.0 g
Saturated Fat	2.0 g
Trans Fat	0.2 g
Cholesterol	80 mg
Sodium	480 mg
Potassium	1000 mg
Total Carbohydrate	11 g
Dietary Fiber	3 g
Sugars	5 g
Protein	27 g
Phosphorus	325 mg

This rich, spicy stew can be served in a bowl or folded into a low-carb whole-wheat burrito. Sometimes I start with a 1/2 cup of stew and top it with beans, salsa, and a lot of fresh garnish.

2 lb boneless beef top sirloin roast, cut into 1-inch cubes
1/4 cup canola oil or mild olive oil
1 large onion, chopped
3 cups chopped Roasted Green Chiles (page 152)
1 (28-oz) can no-salt-added diced tomatoes with juice (see Note)
4 cloves garlic, minced
1 1/2 tsp kosher salt
1 Tbsp coarsely ground black pepper

1. Place beef chunks in a large pot, and add enough water to just cover the beef. Bring to a boil over medium-high heat. Cook uncovered, stirring occasionally, until meat is evenly browned and water and juices have evaporated, about 45 minutes to 1 hour. Remove from heat.
2. In a medium-sized saucepan, sauté onions in oil over medium heat until soft, 8–10 minutes.
3. Slowly add chiles and tomatoes with juice, and boil gently, stirring occasionally until heated through, almost 30 minutes.
4. Add chile mixture to meat. Stir in garlic, salt, and pepper. Continue to simmer, stirring occasionally and adjusting heat as necessary, until stew is thickened, 1–2 hours.

Note: For a thinner saucy stew, add 1 cup water during Step 4.

Tex-Mex Chile con Carne

Real Tex-Mex Chile is full of beef and chile. That is it! Powerful flavor that is addicting. Serve this in a bowl, or ladle it across enchiladas or burritos. It's a Tex-Mex classic.

1 lb lean top sirloin, cubed
1 tsp garlic powder
1 tsp onion powder
1 tsp ground cumin
3 Tbsp chili powder
1 cup water
1 cup Red Chile Purée (page 66)

1. Place beef chunks in a large pot, and add enough water to just cover the beef. Bring to a boil over medium-high heat. Cook uncovered, stirring occasionally, until meat is evenly browned and water and juices have evaporated, about 20–30 minutes. Remove from heat.
2. Add garlic powder, onion powder, cumin, and chili powder, and blend until meat is well coated.
3. Reduce heat to medium-low. Add water and Red Chile Purée. Boil gently, stirring often, until well blended and heated through.

Variations:
- Omit top sirloin. Add 1 lb ground beef and skip Step 1. In a large skillet over medium heat, cook ground beef, breaking up with a spoon, until meat is browned and no longer pink, 10–12 minutes. Drain off excess fat. Follow Steps 2 and 3.
- For more fiber, add 1 (15-oz) can chili beans, rinsed.

Serves: 6
Serving Size: 1/2 cup
Prep Time: 10 minutes
Cook Time: 1 hour

Choices/Exchanges
1 Nonstarchy Vegetable,
2 Lean Protein

Basic Nutritional Values

Calories	130
Calories from Fat	35
Total Fat	4.0 g
Saturated Fat	1.1 g
Trans Fat	0.1 g
Cholesterol	50 mg
Sodium	95 mg
Potassium	470 mg
Total Carbohydrate	6 g
Dietary Fiber	3 g
Sugars	2 g
Protein	18 g
Phosphorus	190 mg

Tostadas, Tacos, Tamales, Burritos, Enchiladas, and More

Here you will find a classic collection of your soon-to-be-favorite Southwestern and Mexican dishes—prepared in easy, delicious, healthy ways. Roasted meats, lentils and beans, fresh veggies, seafood and fish, rich cheeses, and herbs and spices are the foundation for my Tex-Mex tacos, tamales, burritos, and enchiladas.

Tostadas

Frijoles Tostadas 103
Roasted Sweet Potato Tostadas 104
Ceviche Tostadas 105
Chile con Carne Tostadas 107

Tacos

Fajita Tacos 108
Classic Crispy Tacos 109
Classic Rolled Tacos 110
Grilled Carne Asada Tacos 111
Seared Sirloin Tacos with Guacamole 112
Tacos al Pastor 113
Pork Carnitas Tacos 114
Chipotle BBQ Pork Soft Tacos 115
Speedy Roasted Chicken Soft Tacos 116
Chicken Tacos Verde 117
Grilled Mesquite Chicken Tacos 118
Quick Turkey Club Tacos 119
Poblano and Potato Tacos with Chile
    Cream Sauce 120
Spicy Black Bean Tacos 121
Avocado Corn Soft Tacos 122

Crispy Zucchini Tacos 123
Tex-Mex Shrimp Tacos 125
South Texas Fish Tacos 126
Grilled Halibut Tacos 127
No-Beef Taquitos 128
Veggie Taquitos 129
Sweet Potato Taquitos 130
Baked Chicken Flautas 131
Bean and Rice Flautas 132

Tamales

Smoked Cheddar Cheese and Green
    Chile Tamales 133
    Sidebar:
        Tamale Preparation 134
Spinach Asparagus Tamales 135
Red Chile Tamales 137

Burritos

Fiber-Full Burrito Bowls 138
Machaca Burritos 139
Chile Verde Burritos 141
Bean and Cheese Chimichangas 142

Enchiladas

Cheesy Green Chile Enchiladas 143

Tex-Mex Cheese Enchiladas. 145

Sour Cream Green Chile Enchiladas. 146

Red Chile Beefy Street Enchiladas 147

Stacked Saucy Enchiladas with Fresh Greens 148

And More

Torta de Fresco (Mexican Sandwich) 149

Baked Chile Rellenos 150

Savory Stuffed Sopapillas 151

Sidebars:

  Roasted Green Chiles 152

  Shredded Beef 153

  Red Chile Pork 154

  Shredded Chicken. 155

  Tex-Mex Shrimp 156

Tostadas

Frijoles Tostadas

A tostada is like an open-faced taco: beans, chicken, beef, or shrimp layered with rich cheese and fresh greens on a crispy corn tortilla shell. Messy but fun to eat!

1 1/2 cups Refried Beans (page 165) or store-bought reduced-fat refried beans in a brand of your choice, warmed
8 (6-inch) Baked Tostada Shells (page 74) or store-bought reduced-fat tostada shells in a brand of your choice
2 cups Shredded Chicken (page 155) (see Note)
1 cup (about 4 oz) shredded reduced-fat cheddar cheese
2 cups chopped romaine lettuce or shredded iceberg lettuce
1 tomato, seeded and chopped
2 green onions, mostly green part, minced

1. Divide warmed beans equally among tostada shells, spreading to the edge of each shell.
2. Top with equal amounts of chicken, cheese, and lettuce. Garnish with tomato and onion.

Note: For beef Frijoles Tostadas, substitute 2 cups Shredded Beef (page 153) for the chicken. For shrimp Frijoles Tostadas, substitute 2 cups chopped Tex-Mex Shrimp (page 156) for the chicken.

Serves: 8
Serving Size: 1 tostada
Prep Time: 15 minutes
Cook Time: N/A

Choices/Exchanges
1 1/2 Starch, 4 Lean Protein

Basic Nutritional Values

Calories	280
Calories from Fat	70
Total Fat	8.0 g
Saturated Fat	3.2 g
Trans Fat	0.0 g
Cholesterol	60 mg
Sodium	330 mg
Potassium	510 mg
Total Carbohydrate	25 g
Dietary Fiber	5 g
Sugars	1 g
Protein	28 g
Phosphorus	305 mg

Roasted Sweet Potato Tostadas

Serves: 8
Serving Size: 1 tostada
Prep Time: 15 minutes
Cook Time: 40 minutes

Choices/Exchanges

1 Starch, 1 Fat

Basic Nutritional Values

Calories	130
Calories from Fat	45
Total Fat	5.0 g
Saturated Fat	1.8 g
Trans Fat	0.1 g
Cholesterol	10 mg
Sodium	240 mg
Potassium	220 mg
Total Carbohydrate	19 g
Dietary Fiber	3 g
Sugars	3 g
Protein	4 g
Phosphorus	85 mg

Roasted vegetables make a wonderful filling for tostadas. Roasted sweet potatoes layered with herbs and seasonings elevate this tostada's flavor.

2 medium-sized sweet potatoes, peeled and diced
1 Tbsp olive oil
1/8 tsp kosher salt
1/2 tsp chili powder
1/2 tsp garlic powder
1 tsp minced fresh herbs (see Note)
8 (6-inch) Baked Tostada Shells (page 74) or store-bought reduced-fat tostada shells in a brand of your choice
1/2 cup crumbled cotija or feta cheese
2 cups chopped fresh mixed greens or romaine lettuce
1/2 cup thinly sliced red onion

1. Preheat oven to 425°F and place the rack in the center of the oven.
2. In a medium-sized, bowl toss sweet potatoes with oil, salt, chili powder, garlic powder, and herbs. Pour onto a baking sheet and roast for 30–40 minutes, using a spatula to stir and turn potatoes occasionally until they're soft yet crispy.
3. To build the tostadas, divide sweet potatoes equally among tostada shells.
4. Top with equal amounts of cheese and greens. Garnish with onion.

Note: I like flat-leaf parsley. For a more intense flavor, add fresh cilantro.

Ceviche Tostadas

White fish fillet makes this tostada fresh and simple. The chile and citrus give it depth of flavor.

- 1 cup Refried Beans (page 165) or store-bought reduced-fat refried beans in a brand of your choice, warmed
- 8 (6-inch) Baked Tostada Shells (page 74) or store-bought reduced-fat tostada shells in a brand of your choice
- 2 cups Ceviche (page 22)
- 1 1/2 cups leafy greens, torn into bite-size pieces
- 1 avocado, seeded and diced

1. To build the tostadas, divide warmed beans equally among tostada shells, spreading to the edge of each shell.
2. Top each tostada with equal amounts of Ceviche and greens. Garnish with avocado.

Serves: 8
Serving Size: 1 tostada
Prep Time: 10 minutes
Cook Time: N/A

Choices/Exchanges
1 Starch, 1/2 Carbohydrate, 1 Lean Protein, 1 Fat

Basic Nutritional Values

Calories	200
Calories from Fat	50
Total Fat	6.0 g
Saturated Fat	1.2 g
Trans Fat	0.0 g
Cholesterol	10 mg
Sodium	230 mg
Potassium	590 mg
Total Carbohydrate	26 g
Dietary Fiber	6 g
Sugars	2 g
Protein	11 g
Phosphorus	175 mg

Chile con Carne Tostadas

Tex-Mex Chile con Carne (page 99) goes on everything! These saucy tostadas are rich in flavor, and they're very filling.

2 cups Tex-Mex Chile con Carne (page 99), warmed
8 (6-inch) Baked Tostada Shells (page 74) or store-bought reduced-fat tostada shells in a brand of your choice
1 cup (about 4 oz) shredded reduced-fat cheddar cheese
1/2 cup chopped onion
2 cups shredded iceberg lettuce

1. Divide Tex-Mex Chile con Carne equally among tostada shells, spreading to the edge of each shell.
2. Top with equal amounts of cheese, onion, and lettuce. Serve immediately.

Serves: 8
Serving Size: 1 tostada
Prep Time: 10 minutes
Cook Time: N/A

Choices/Exchanges
1 Starch, 1 Lean Protein, 1/2 Fat

Basic Nutritional Values

Calories	140
Calories from Fat	45
Total Fat	5.0 g
Saturated Fat	2.2 g
Trans Fat	0.0 g
Cholesterol	20 mg
Sodium	240 mg
Potassium	210 mg
Total Carbohydrate	15 g
Dietary Fiber	3 g
Sugars	1 g
Protein	10 g
Phosphorus	170 mg

Tacos

Fajita Tacos

Serves: 8
Serving Size: 1 taco
Prep Time: 20 minutes
Cook Time: 20 minutes

Choices/Exchanges

1 Starch, 1 Nonstarchy
Vegetable, 2 Lean Protein,
1 1/2 Fat

Basic Nutritional Values

Calories	260
Calories from Fat	120
Total Fat	13.0 g
Saturated Fat	4.8 g
Trans Fat	0.0 g
Cholesterol	30 mg
Sodium	350 mg
Potassium	470 mg
Total Carbohydrate	21 g
Dietary Fiber	3 g
Sugars	4 g
Protein	16 g
Phosphorus	245 mg

Fajita-style dining is true Tex-Mex! Sizzling beef, chicken, or shrimp screams Tex-Mex! Pile it high with all the fixin's for a great taco dinner.

1 lb lean (visible fat removed) beef skirt steak (see Note)
1/4 tsp kosher salt
2 Tbsp olive oil, divided use
1 onion, sliced into 1/4-inch rings
1 red bell pepper, julienned
1 orange bell pepper, julienned
Freshly ground black pepper
8 (6-inch) corn or low-carb flour tortillas, warmed (page 75)
1/2 cup fat-free sour cream
1 cup (about 4 oz) shredded reduced-fat cheddar or Monterey Jack cheese
1 cup Pico de Gallo (page 48)
2 limes, each cut into 4 wedges

1. Season steak with salt on both sides. In a large skillet, heat 1 Tbsp of oil over medium heat. Sear steak on both sides until juices come to the surface and steak has a medium pink center (4–6 minutes per side). Transfer to a cutting board, and slice into 1/4-inch strips.
2. Add remaining oil to skillet, and sauté onion and red and orange bell peppers until peppers are tender-crisp and all vegetables are slightly charred, about 10–12 minutes. Add sliced steak, season with black pepper, toss with vegetables, and heat through.
3. To build the tacos, divide meat mixture equally among tortillas and fold tortillas in half. Serve with sour cream, cheese, Pico de Gallo, and lime wedges.

Note: For chicken Fajita Tacos, substitute split chicken breasts (about 1 lb) for skirt steak. In a large skillet, heat 1 Tbsp oil over medium heat. Sauté chicken until no longer pink inside and juices have evaporated, 12–14 minutes. Remove chicken from skillet, slice into 1/4-inch strips, and set aside. Follow Steps 2 and 3.

Classic Crispy Tacos

In Tex-Mex cooking, the taco has evolved into many versions. However, the Classic Crispy Taco is always a hit. Enjoy a savory filling layered with creamy cheese and veggies.

3 cups Shredded Chicken (page 155), warmed
1/2 tsp salt
1/2 tsp black pepper
8 folded taco shells (see Note)
2 cups shredded iceberg lettuce
1 cup (about 4 oz) shredded reduced-fat cheddar cheese
1 medium onion, minced
1 large tomato, seeded and diced

1. In a large bowl, toss chicken with salt and pepper.
2. To build the tacos, divide chicken equally among the taco shells. Top each taco equally with lettuce, cheese, onion, and tomato.

Note: For a reduced-fat version, use 8 (6-inch) Fresh Corn Tortillas (page 72), skillet-warmed (page 75), for soft, folded taco shells.

Variation: Omit Shredded Chicken and add 1 lb lean ground beef, cooked and drained. Follow Steps 1 and 2.

Serves: 8
Serving Size: 1 taco
Prep Time: 15 minutes
Cook Time: N/A

Choices/Exchanges
1 Starch, 4 Lean Protein

Basic Nutritional Values

Calories	250
Calories from Fat	60
Total Fat	7.0 g
Saturated Fat	2.7 g
Trans Fat	0.0 g
Cholesterol	80 mg
Sodium	420 mg
Potassium	330 mg
Total Carbohydrate	15 g
Dietary Fiber	2 g
Sugars	2 g
Protein	33 g
Phosphorus	285 mg

Classic Rolled Tacos

Serves: 24

Serving Size: 1 taco

Prep Time: 30 minutes

Chill Time: 2 hours

Cook Time: 15 minutes

Choices/Exchanges

1 Starch, 1 Lean Protein,
1 Fat

Basic Nutritional Values

Calories	150
Calories from Fat	80
Total Fat	9.0 g
Saturated Fat	1.1 g
Trans Fat	0.1 g
Cholesterol	20 mg
Sodium	210 mg
Potassium	110 mg
Total Carbohydrate	12 g
Dietary Fiber	2 g
Sugars	0 g
Protein	7 g
Phosphorus	75 mg

Rolled tacos, or "taquitos"—special flute-like creations—are a treat to be eaten in moderation. I like to skillet-fry them instead of deep-frying them; this will garner the same texture with fewer calories.

2 cups Shredded Beef (page 153) (see Variations)
3/4 tsp salt
24 (6-inch) Fresh Corn Tortillas (page 72), micro-warmed (page 75)
3/4 cup vegetable oil

1. In a large bowl, thoroughly combine Shredded Beef and salt.
2. To build the tacos, place about 1 1/2 Tbsp meat at one end of each tortilla. Gently roll tortilla and secure with a toothpick. Place rolled tacos in a resealable plastic bag to set and keep moist. Refrigerate sealed bag for at least 2 hours or up to 2 days.
3. When ready to cook, add 2 Tbsp oil to a deep skillet over medium-high heat. Using tongs, gently place 3–4 tacos at a time in the hot oil, turning once until golden brown and crispy, 2–3 minutes. Drain on paper towels. Repeat for the remaining tacos, using 2 Tbsp of oil at a time.

Variations:
- No-Fry Rolled Tacos: Follow Steps 1–2. When ready to cook, preheat oven to 400°F. Spray a sheet pan with cooking spray. Remove rolled tacos from resealable bag one at a time. Place the tacos seam side down on the pan, and spray them lightly with cooking spray. Bake for 20 minutes, until golden brown and crispy. Drain on paper towels.
- Chicken Rolled Tacos: Omit Shredded Beef, and add 2 cups Shredded Chicken (page 155). Follow Steps 2–3.

Grilled Carne Asada Tacos

The intense flavor of this taco comes from an easy-to-make marinade. Grilling gives the filling a charred texture that adds to the flavor.

1/2 cup light teriyaki sauce
Juice of 2 lemons
2 cloves garlic, minced
1/2 cup drained, sliced, pickled jalapeño pepper
1 Tbsp zero-calorie granulated sweetener (such as Splenda)
2 tsp kosher salt
1 1/2 lb beef skirt steak or minute steak
8 (6-inch) Fresh Corn Tortillas (page 72), micro-warmed (page 75)
1 cup Pico de Gallo (page 48)
2 limes, each cut into 4 wedges

1. In a medium-sized bowl, combine teriyaki sauce, lemon juice, garlic, jalapeños, zero-calorie granulated sweetener, and salt. Stir marinade until well blended.
2. In a large resealable plastic bag, add marinade and meat. Seal the bag and work the marinade through the meat with your hands. Refrigerate meat for at least 2 hours or for up to 6 hours.
3. Preheat greased barbecue grill to medium. Remove meat from marinade, and discard remaining marinade.
4. Grill meat for 5–7 minutes per side for medium doneness. When meat is just barely pink inside, remove from grill. Let stand for 8–10 minutes. Carve meat across the grain into thin slices, then cut into bite-size pieces.
5. To build the tacos, skillet-warm the tortillas (page 75). Divide meat equally among tortillas, and top each with 2 Tbsp Pico de Gallo. Fold tortillas in half. Serve with a wedge of lime.

Variation: In a large skillet over medium heat, sear meat for 5–6 minutes on each side, turning once, until barely pink inside. Let stand for 8–10 minutes. Carve meat across the grain into thin slices, then cut into bite-size pieces.

Serves: 8
Serving Size: 1 taco
Prep Time: 10 minutes
Chill Time: 2 hours
Cook Time: 14 minutes

Choices/Exchanges

1 Starch, 1 Nonstarchy Vegetable, 2 Lean Protein, 1/2 Fat

Basic Nutritional Values

Calories	220
Calories from Fat	70
Total Fat	8.0 g
Saturated Fat	2.7 g
Trans Fat	0.3 g
Cholesterol	55 mg
Sodium	410 mg
Potassium	390 mg
Total Carbohydrate	17 g
Dietary Fiber	2 g
Sugars	3 g
Protein	20 g
Phosphorus	160 mg

Seared Sirloin Tacos with Guacamole

Serves: 8
Serving Size: 1 taco
Prep Time: 12 minutes
Cook Time: 8 minutes

Basic Nutritional Values

Calories	190
Calories from Fat	60
Total Fat	7.0 g
Saturated Fat	1.7 g
Trans Fat	0.1 g
Cholesterol	30 mg
Sodium	430 mg
Potassium	380 mg
Total Carbohydrate	15 g
Dietary Fiber	2 g
Sugars	1 g
Protein	19 g
Phosphorus	180 mg

This is a Mexican favorite full of tender meat seared to perfection. Topped with the fresh flavors of avocado and Pico de Gallo, this simple taco is authentic and delicious.

1 1/2 lb boneless beef sirloin steak, cut into bite-size pieces
1 1/2 tsp seasoned salt
1/2 tsp garlic powder
1 Tbsp olive oil
8 (6-inch) Fresh Corn Tortillas (page 72), warmed (page 75)
1/2 cup Fresh Green Chile Guacamole (page 48)
1 cup Pico de Gallo (page 48)
2 limes, each cut into 4 wedges

1. In a large bowl combine meat with salt and garlic powder. Toss until well coated.
2. In a large skillet, heat oil over medium-high heat. Sauté meat until all juices have evaporated and meat is slightly charred, about 8–10 minutes.
3. To build the tacos, divide meat equally among tortillas. Top each with 1 Tbsp guacamole and 2 Tbsp Pico de Gallo. Fold tortillas in half. Serve with fresh lime wedges.

Tacos al Pastor

Tacos al Pastor, also known as the shepherd's taco from its Middle Eastern roots and the Mexican street vendors, has a sweet/spicy–flavored filling. Pork infused with spicy, smoky chiles and pineapple is inviting and delicious.

1 Tbsp olive oil
1 lb pork tenderloin, cut into 1/2-inch cubes
1 onion, chopped, divided use
1/2 cup canned pineapple chunks, drained, with 1/3 cup juice reserved
4 chipotle chile peppers in adobo sauce
12 (6-inch) Fresh Corn Tortillas (page 72), warmed (page 75)
2 Tbsp minced cilantro
1 1/2 cups Pico de Gallo (page 48)
3 limes, cut into wedges

1. In a large skillet, heat oil to medium-high and add pork and half of the onion. Sauté until juices have cooked away and pork is crispy on the the surface, about 20 minutes.
2. In food processor, purée pineapple, remaining onion, and chiles until smooth. Add about 1/3 cup pineapple juice to thin out the purée.
3. Add the purée to the skillet, covering the pork and onions. Simmer over medium-low heat until heated through, about 12 minutes.
4. To build the tacos, divide pork among tortillas. Top with cilantro and Pico de Gallo. Fold tortillas in half. Serve each with a lime wedge.

Serves: 12
Serving Size: 1 taco
Prep Time: 20 minutes
Cook Time: 35 minutes

Choices/Exchanges

1 Starch, 1 Nonstarchy Vegetable, 1 Lean Protein

Basic Nutritional Values

Calories	140
Calories from Fat	25
Total Fat	3.0 g
Saturated Fat	0.6 g
Trans Fat	0.0 g
Cholesterol	20 mg
Sodium	160 mg
Potassium	350 mg
Total Carbohydrate	19 g
Dietary Fiber	3 g
Sugars	4 g
Protein	10 g
Phosphorus	125 mg

Pork Carnitas Tacos

Serves: 16
Serving Size: 1 taco
Prep Time: 20 minutes
Cook Time: 3 1/2 hours

Choices/Exchanges

1 Starch, 1 Lean Protein, 1/2 Fat

Basic Nutritional Values

Calories	150
Calories from Fat	50
Total Fat	6.0 g
Saturated Fat	1.8 g
Trans Fat	0.0 g
Cholesterol	30 mg
Sodium	210 mg
Potassium	220 mg
Total Carbohydrate	15 g
Dietary Fiber	2 g
Sugars	1 g
Protein	11 g
Phosphorus	120 mg

These classic pork tacos can be garnished in many ways. The flavor of the pork filling is strong and mixes well with many flavors. Team it with Roasted Tomatillo Chile Sauce (page 50) for a citrusy finish, Spicy Corn Salsa (page 52) for a rich earthy flavor, or Roasted Pineapple Salsa (page 57) for a sweeter accent.

2 lb boneless pork shoulder blade roast (butt), cubed
1 large onion, sliced
2 cloves garlic, chopped
1 Tbsp kosher salt
2 medium onions, diced
4 fresh serrano or jalapeño peppers, seeded and chopped
16 (6-inch) Fresh Corn Tortillas (page 72)
4 fresh limes, cut into quarter wedges

1. Place pork in a large pot, and add just enough water to just cover the pork. Add onion, garlic, and salt, and bring to a boil over medium-high heat. Reduce heat to medium-low, cover pot, and boil gently until pork is tender, 2–3 hours.
2. Remove pork from pot, reserving 1 cup of liquid. Let pork cool. Shred with two forks or chop into tiny pieces, discarding excess fat.
3. Coat a large skillet lightly with cooking spray, and add a couple tablespoons reserved cooking liquid. Over medium heat, sauté onions and peppers until tender, 4–6 minutes. Add pork and remaining reserved liquid. Cook over medium-high heat, stirring, until all juices have evaporated, about 15 minutes.
4. To build the tacos, divide pork mixture equally among warmed tortillas. Fold tortillas in half to create a half-moon shape. Serve each with a fresh lime wedge.

Chipotle BBQ Pork Soft Tacos

Texas loves barbecue! This family-style taco is fun for the whole gang!

2 cloves garlic, minced
1 cup reduced-sugar barbecue sauce, in a store-bought brand of your choice
4 chipotle chile peppers in adobo sauce, puréed
2 lb boneless pork shoulder blade (butt) roast, trimmed
1 1/2 tsp hot smoked paprika
16 (6-inch to 7-inch) low-carb whole-wheat flour tortillas
2 cups shredded cabbage
1 1/2 cups diced onion (about 2 medium onions)

1. In a medium-sized bowl, combine minced garlic, barbecue sauce, and puréed chipotle peppers. Blend well. Set aside.
2. Place pork in a 3–6-quart slow-cooker. Cover and cook on low for 8–10 hours or on high for 4–6 hours. Transfer pork to a cutting board. Shred pork with two forks, discarding excess fat. Return pork to slow-cooker.
3. Sprinkle paprika over shredded pork. Add barbecue mixture. Cover and cook on low for 1 hour to infuse flavors. Skim off any excess fat.
4. To build the tacos, place heaping spoonfuls of pork on warmed tortillas, and top with cabbage and onion. Fold the tortillas in half.

Serves: 16
Serving Size: 1 taco
Prep Time: 15 minutes
Cook Time: 4–6 hours on high or 8–10 hours on low plus 1 additional hour

Choices/Exchanges
1/2 Starch,
1/2 Carbohydrate,
2 Lean Protein, 1/2 Fat

Basic Nutritional Values

Calories	160
Calories from Fat	60
Total Fat	7.0 g
Saturated Fat	1.9 g
Trans Fat	0.0 g
Cholesterol	30 mg
Sodium	350 mg
Potassium	230 mg
Total Carbohydrate	15 g
Dietary Fiber	8 g
Sugars	3 g
Protein	15 g
Phosphorus	130 mg

Speedy Roasted Chicken Soft Tacos

Serves: 8
Serving Size: 1 taco
Prep Time: 15 minutes
Cook Time: N/A

Choices/Exchanges

1 Starch, 2 Lean Protein, 1 Fat

Basic Nutritional Values

Calories	200
Calories from Fat	90
Total Fat	10.0 g
Saturated Fat	2.3 g
Trans Fat	0.0 g
Cholesterol	45 mg
Sodium	280 mg
Potassium	390 mg
Total Carbohydrate	17 g
Dietary Fiber	4 g
Sugars	1 g
Protein	14 g
Phosphorus	180 mg

Market-fresh rotisserie chicken is tempting for weekday dinners when life gets rushed. The chicken can be high in sodium, so I limit the amount I put in a recipe and mix it with lots of veggies.

1 cup chopped romaine lettuce
1 cup chopped fresh spinach
1/2 cup minced red onion
1 Tbsp rice vinegar
2 cups shredded rotisserie chicken, skin removed and discarded
8 (6-inch) Fresh Corn Tortillas (page 72), warmed (page 75)
2 ripe avocados, diced
1/2 cup (about 2 oz) shredded reduced-fat Monterey Jack cheese

1. In a medium-sized bowl, combine lettuce, spinach, red onion, and rice vinegar.
2. To build the tacos, divide chicken equally among tortillas; top with lettuce mixture, avocados, and cheese; and fold tortillas in half.

Chicken Tacos Verde

Green chile is the perfect match with chicken, and the chicken and chile flavors in this taco blend well with the citrusy flavor of the tomatillo salsa.

1 Tbsp olive oil
1/2 cup minced onion
1/3 cup fresh chopped green chile
1 Tbsp water
2 cups Shredded Chicken (page 155)
1/2 tsp salt
8 (6-inch) Fresh Corn Tortillas (page 72), warmed (page 75)
1 cup Roasted Tomatillo Chile Sauce (page 50) or store-bought green chile sauce in a brand of your choice
1 cup (about 4 oz) shredded reduced-fat Monterey Jack cheese

1. Preheat the broiler.
2. In a large skillet, heat oil over medium heat. Add onion and sauté until soft, about 4 minutes. Add green chile and water, and cook until mixture is heated through and onion is translucent, about 6 minutes. Add chicken and salt. Blend well and heat through.
3. To build the tacos, divide chicken mixture among tortillas on individual ovenproof plates. Top with sauce and cheese. Broil until cheese melts. Fold tortillas in half and serve immediately.

Serves: 8
Serving Size: 1 taco
Prep Time: 30 minutes
Cook Time: 14 minutes

Choices/Exchanges
1 Starch, 3 Lean Protein

Basic Nutritional Values

Calories	220
Calories from Fat	70
Total Fat	8.0 g
Saturated Fat	2.7 g
Trans Fat	0.0 g
Cholesterol	60 mg
Sodium	440 mg
Potassium	310 mg
Total Carbohydrate	16 g
Dietary Fiber	2 g
Sugars	2 g
Protein	24 g
Phosphorus	220 mg

Grilled Mesquite Chicken Tacos

Serves: 8
Serving Size: 1 taco
Prep Time: 10 minutes
Chill Time: 2 hours
Cook Time: 16 minutes

Choices/Exchanges

1 Starch, 1/2 Carbohydrate,
2 Lean Protein, 1/2 Fat

Basic Nutritional Values

Calories	210
Calories from Fat	70
Total Fat	8.0 g
Saturated Fat	3.2 g
Trans Fat	0.0 g
Cholesterol	40 mg
Sodium	300 mg
Potassium	230 mg
Total Carbohydrate	20 g
Dietary Fiber	3 g
Sugars	4 g
Protein	16 g
Phosphorus	210 mg

Grilling over mesquite wood is customary across Texas. Smoky mesquite flavor can be infused in everyday cooking through high-quality seasonings. That's what this taco is all about.

Juice of 2 limes
2 Tbsp mesquite seasoning (see Note)
1 Tbsp honey
1 Tbsp olive oil
3 (about 12-oz) boneless, skinless chicken breasts
8 (6-inch) Fresh Corn Tortillas (page 72), warmed (page 75)
1 cup Spicy Corn Salsa (page 52)
2 cups chopped mixed greens
1 1/2 cups (about 6 oz) shredded reduced-fat Monterey Jack

1. In a small bowl, combine lime juice, mesquite seasoning, honey, and olive oil. Mix well.
2. In a resealable plastic bag, combine marinade and chicken. Seal the bag and work the marinade into the chicken with your hands. Refrigerate for at least 2 hours or up to 4 hours.
3. Preheat greased barbecue grill to medium-high.
4. Remove chicken from marinade and discard remaining marinade.
5. Grill chicken, turning once, until no longer pink inside and juices run clear (about 6–8 minutes per side). Transfer chicken to a cutting board and let stand for 6–8 minutes, then cut into bite-size pieces.
6. To build the tacos, divide chicken equally among tortillas. Top with salsa, greens, and cheese. Fold tortillas in half.

Note: Mesquite seasoning adds an earthy essence to grilled chicken. Try the different mesquite seasonings at your local grocery store to find your favorite.

Quick Turkey Club Tacos

This panini-style taco is packed with flavor. The grilled turkey and jalapeño cheese blend well, creating a lunch-style taco you will love.

Butter-flavored cooking spray
16 slices roasted low-sodium deli turkey, chopped
8 (6-inch or 8-inch) flour tortillas
8 thin slices reduced-fat jalapeño cheese
8 strips turkey bacon, cooked and crumbled
2 large tomatoes, thinly sliced
2 cups shredded iceberg lettuce

1. Coat a large skillet lightly with cooking spray.
2. Sauté the turkey over medium-high heat until slightly charred, about 3-4 minutes. Remove from the skillet and set aside.
3. Place one tortilla in the skillet, and cook over medium heat until air bubbles begin to form, about 1 minute.
4. Place one slice of cheese in the center of the tortilla. Top with 1 strip of crumbled bacon, 1/8 of the turkey, and 2-3 slices of tomato. Cook until the cheese starts to melt, about 1 minute.
5. Fold tortilla in half to create a half-moon shape. Flip folded tortilla over, and cook until tortilla is lightly toasted and cheese filling is completely melted, 1-2 minutes.
6. Transfer taco to a serving platter. Recoat the skillet with cooking spray and repeat.
7. Just before serving, pull each tortilla open and add 2 Tbsp shredded lettuce. Serve immediately with Classic Guacamole (page 29) and a favorite salsa (optional).

Serves: 8
Serving Size: 1 taco
Prep Time: 10 minutes
Cook Time: 36 minutes

Choices/Exchanges
1 1/2 Starch,
2 Lean Protein, 1 Fat

Basic Nutritional Values

Calories.................260
  Calories from Fat.........90
Total Fat.............10.0 g
  Saturated Fat..........3.3 g
  Trans Fat..............0.0 g
Cholesterol...........35 mg
Sodium...............480 mg
Potassium...........340 mg
Total Carbohydrate.......25 g
  Dietary Fiber...........3 g
  Sugars................2 g
Protein................19 g
Phosphorus..........265 mg

Poblano and Potato Tacos with Chile Cream Sauce

Serves: 8
Serving Size: 1 taco
Prep Time: 15 minutes
Cook Time: 20 minutes

Choices/Exchanges
1 1/2 Starch, 1/2 Fat

Basic Nutritional Values

Calories	130
Calories from Fat	35
Total Fat	4.0 g
Saturated Fat	0.7 g
Trans Fat	0.0 g
Cholesterol	4 mg
Sodium	270 mg
Potassium	300 mg
Total Carbohydrate	22 g
Dietary Fiber	3 g
Sugars	3 g
Protein	3 g
Phosphorus	90 mg

A corn tortilla piled high with a sweet, spicy filling makes a supreme veggie taco. Layers of spice add flavor to the sweet potato filling.

1 Tbsp olive oil
2 cups peeled, diced sweet potatoes
1/2 cup diced onion
1 cup chopped roasted poblano chile
3 Tbsp freshly grated parmesan cheese
1/2 tsp chipotle pepper powder (see Note)
8 (6-inch) Fresh Corn Tortillas (page 72), warmed (page 75)
1/2 cup Chile Cream Sauce (page 60)

1. In a large skillet, heat oil over medium-high heat. Add sweet potatoes, cover, and cook until soft, about 8–10 minutes. Remove the lid and cook, stirring occasionally, until potatoes are golden brown and crispy, 8–10 minutes.
2. Lightly coat another skillet with cooking spray, gently add onion and chile, and sauté until soft, about 4–6 minutes.
3. In a large bowl, combine parmesan and chipotle powder. Add warm potatoes and onion mixture. Toss to coat. Season with salt (optional).
4. To build the tacos, divide potato mixture equally among tortillas. Top evenly with Chile Cream Sauce. Fold tortillas in half.

Note: For a different chile flavor, substitute cayenne pepper.

Spicy Black Bean Tacos

These hearty tacos are full of fiber and quite filling. They are quick and easy to make, too.

- 2 cloves garlic, minced
- 1 Tbsp olive oil
- 2 1/2 cups rinsed drained canned black beans
- 1 tsp crushed red pepper flakes
- 1/2 tsp salt
- 8 (6-inch) Fresh Corn Tortillas (page 72), warmed (page 75)
- 2 cups chopped leafy greens
- 1/2 cup Pickled Onions (page 55)

1. In a large skillet, sauté garlic in oil over medium heat for 1–2 minutes. Add beans, red pepper flakes, and salt. Cook until heated through.
2. To build the tacos, divide bean mixture equally among tortillas. Top with greens and onions.

Serves: 8
Serving Size: 1 taco
Prep Time: 10 minutes
Cook Time: 5 minutes

Choices/Exchanges

1 1/2 Starch, 1 Nonstarchy Vegetable

Basic Nutritional Values

Calories	150
Calories from Fat	20
Total Fat	2.5 g
Saturated Fat	0.4 g
Trans Fat	0.0 g
Cholesterol	0 mg
Sodium	420 mg
Potassium	290 mg
Total Carbohydrate	27 g
Dietary Fiber	7 g
Sugars	2 g
Protein	7 g
Phosphorus	115 mg

Avocado Corn Soft Tacos

Serves: 8

Serving Size: 1 taco

Prep Time: 10 minutes

Cook Time: 5 minutes

Choices/Exchanges
1 Starch, 1/2 Carbohydrate, 2 Fat

Basic Nutritional Values

Calories	190
Calories from Fat	90
Total Fat	10.0 g
Saturated Fat	2.5 g
Trans Fat	0.0 g
Cholesterol	10 mg
Sodium	240 mg
Potassium	350 mg
Total Carbohydrate	22 g
Dietary Fiber	5 g
Sugars	3 g
Protein	5 g
Phosphorus	135 mg

Grilled corn and onion make a delightful veggie filling for this taco. The chipotle seasoning really comes through with a smoky chile accent.

1 Tbsp olive oil
1 tsp chipotle pepper powder
1/2 tsp garlic powder
1/8 tsp kosher salt
2 medium onions, thinly sliced
1 cup corn kernels
8 (6-inch) Fresh Corn Tortillas (page 72), warmed (page 75)
1/2 cup crumbled cotija or feta cheese
2 avocados, peeled and diced

1. Preheat broiler.
2. In a medium-sized bowl, combine olive oil, chipotle powder, garlic powder, and kosher salt. Add onions and corn. Toss until well coated.
3. Pour corn mixture on a baking sheet, spreading out to a thin layer. Broil for 3–4 minutes. Remove from broiler and use a spatula to turn vegetables. Broil for an additional 2–3 minutes, until mixture is slightly charred.
4. To build the tacos, divide corn mixture equally among tortillas. Top with cheese and avocados. Fold tortillas in half.

Crispy Zucchini Tacos

Crispy taco shells filled with fresh veggies are a delight. This unique combination of fresh zucchini, spicy salsa, and rich creamy cheese is delicioso!

- 1 Tbsp olive oil
- 1 clove garlic, minced
- 3 cups chopped zucchini
- 1 cup Tex-Mex Salsa (page 49) or store-bought chunky tomato salsa in a brand of your choice
- 8 reduced-fat crispy corn tortilla shells, warmed (page 75)
- 1 1/2 cups (about 6 oz) shredded reduced-fat Monterey Jack cheese

1. In a large skillet, heat oil over medium-high heat. Add garlic, zucchini, and salsa, and sauté until zucchini is tender-crisp, 6–8 minutes. Drain off excess liquid.
2. To build the tacos, divide zucchini mixture equally among tortilla shells. Top with cheese.

Serves: 8
Serving Size: 1 taco
Prep Time: 10 minutes
Cook Time: 8 minutes

Choices/Exchanges

1/2 Starch, 1 Nonstarchy Vegetable, 1 Lean Protein, 1 Fat

Basic Nutritional Values

Calories	150
Calories from Fat	60
Total Fat	7.0 g
Saturated Fat	3.0 g
Trans Fat	0.0 g
Cholesterol	15 mg
Sodium	320 mg
Potassium	260 mg
Total Carbohydrate	16 g
Dietary Fiber	2 g
Sugars	2 g
Protein	8 g
Phosphorus	155 mg

Tex-Mex Shrimp Tacos

Light and healthy seafood tacos are so refreshing and fun. Fresh greens and herbs top the delicately spiced shrimp, while the white sauce keeps it all cool.

3 cups Tex-Mex Shrimp (page 156), warmed and chopped
8 (6-inch) Fresh Corn Tortillas (page 72), warmed (page 75)
1 Tbsp chopped fresh cilantro
2 cups chopped mixed greens
1/2 cup Mexican White Sauce (page 53)

1. To build the tacos, divide the Tex-Mex Shrimp equally among the tortillas.
2. Top the tortillas with cilantro and greens, drizzle with sauce, and fold in half.

Serves: 8
Serving Size: 1 taco
Prep Time: 12 minutes
Cook Time: N/A

Choices/Exchanges

1 Starch, 1 Lean Protein

Basic Nutritional Values

Calories. 120
 Calories from Fat 45
Total Fat . . . . .5.0 g
 Saturated Fat . . . . .0.6 g
 Trans Fat . . . . .0.0 g
Cholesterol . . . . 25 mg
Sodium . . . . 230 mg
Potassium . . . . .135 mg
Total Carbohydrate. . . . . . . .15 g
 Dietary Fiber . . . . 2 g
 Sugars. . . . . .1 g
Protein . . . . 5 g
Phosphorus . . . . 85 mg

South Texas Fish Tacos

Serves: 8
Serving Size: 1 taco
Prep Time: 15 minutes
Cook Time: 14 minutes

Choices/Exchanges

1 1/2 Starch, 1 Nonstarchy
Vegetable, 2 Lean Protein

Basic Nutritional Values

Calories	210
Calories from Fat	35
Total Fat	4.0 g
Saturated Fat	0.5 g
Trans Fat	0.0 g
Cholesterol	25 mg
Sodium	460 mg
Potassium	400 mg
Total Carbohydrate	29 g
Dietary Fiber	4 g
Sugars	4 g
Protein	16 g
Phosphorus	160 mg

Fish fillets lightly breaded in panko flakes and baked to perfection make a great taco filling. Layered with a mild sauce and fresh vegetables, these fish tacos are so good!

2 cups whole-wheat panko flakes
3/4 tsp salt
1/2 tsp pepper
2 tsp garlic powder
1 lb skinless cod or tilapia fillets (see Variation)
3 egg whites, beaten
8 (6-inch) Fresh Corn Tortillas (page 72), warmed (page 75)
1/2 cup Mexican White Sauce (page 53) or fat-free sour cream
1 cup thinly shredded red cabbage
1 cup thinly shredded green cabbage
1 cup Pico de Gallo (page 48)

1. In a medium-sized bowl, combine panko flakes, salt, pepper, and garlic powder and mix well.
2. Rinse fish and pat dry with paper towel. Cut into 1/2-inch strips.
3. Pour beaten egg whites into a shallow dish. Dip fish into egg, then coat with panko flake mixture.
4. Place coated fillet pieces on a baking sheet, 1 inch apart. Bake at 400°F for 7 minutes. Turn, then bake for 7 minutes more, until golden brown.
5. To build the tacos, divide the fish equally among each tortilla. Drizzle with Mexican White Sauce, then top evenly with cabbage and Pico de Gallo. Fold tortillas in half.

Variation: For skillet cooking, follow Steps 1–3. Then, lightly coat a large skillet with cooking spray and cook coated fillet pieces over medium-high heat, turning once, until fish flakes easily with a fork (about 4–5 minutes per side). Follow Step 5.

Grilled Halibut Tacos

Halibut is tasty with fresh veggies. Perfect for a fish taco laced with white sauce and marinated onions.

1 1/2 lb halibut steak
1/2 cup Mexican White Sauce (page 53) or reduced-fat mayonnaise
2 Tbsp panko flakes
8 (6-inch) Fresh Corn Tortillas (page 72), warmed (page 75)
1 1/2 cups finely chopped romaine lettuce
1 cup Pickled Onions (page 55)

1. Preheat oven to 450°F.
2. Lightly coat an 8 x 8-inch baking dish with cooking spray.
3. Rinse halibut and pat dry with paper towel. Place in baking dish and bake until fish flakes easily when tested with a fork, 8–10 minutes. Drain excess moisture.
4. Preheat broiler.
5. Spread sauce evenly on top of the halibut steak, covering to the edges. Sprinkle with panko flakes. Broil until crust is golden brown and bubbling, 2–3 minutes.
6. To build the tacos, gently cut halibut into 8 pieces and divide equally among the tortillas. Top with lettuce and Pickled Onions. Fold tortillas in half.

Serves: 8
Serving Size: 1 taco
Prep Time: 12 minutes
Cook Time: 13 minutes

Choices/Exchanges

1 Starch, 3 Lean Protein

Basic Nutritional Values

Calories	200
Calories from Fat	45
Total Fat	5.0 g
Saturated Fat	0.8 g
Trans Fat	0.0 g
Cholesterol	30 mg
Sodium	460 mg
Potassium	510 mg
Total Carbohydrate	18 g
Dietary Fiber	2 g
Sugars	2 g
Protein	20 g
Phosphorus	250 mg

No-Beef Taquitos

Serves: 6
Serving Size: 2 taquitos
Prep Time: 15 minutes
Chill Time: 2 hours
Cook Time: 26 minutes

Choices/Exchanges

2 Starch

Basic Nutritional Values

Calories	150
Calories from Fat	20
Total Fat	2.0 g
Saturated Fat	0.3 g
Trans Fat	0.0 g
Cholesterol	0 mg
Sodium	450 mg
Potassium	160 mg
Total Carbohydrate	27 g
Dietary Fiber	5 g
Sugars	0 g
Protein	7 g
Phosphorus	100 mg

These crispy little taquitos are one of my favorites! You would never know they're meatless. The veggie crumbles—a combination of vegetables, rice, and soy—add a hearty healthiness to the taco filling, which is high in protein and low in fat. Baked or lightly fried, they're a savory treat—as well as simple and economical.

1 cup prepared veggie crumbles (see Note)
2 Tbsp water
3 Tbsp mashed Pinto Beans (page 164)
1/2 tsp salt
12 (6-inch) Fresh Corn Tortillas (page 72), micro-warmed (page 75)
Cooking spray

1. In a skillet over medium-high heat, mix the veggie crumbles with 2 Tbsp water and cook for 4 minutes. Reduce the heat to medium-low and cook another 2–4 minutes, until the crumbles are heated through. Transfer the crumbles to a medium-sized mixing bowl to cool. When the crumbles have cooled, add the mashed Pinto Beans and salt and mix well. The texture will be crumbly and moist.
2. To build the taquitos, place 1–1 1/2 Tbsp filling at one end of each tortilla. Gently roll the tortilla up and secure it with a toothpick. Place the rolled taquitos in a resealable plastic bag and refrigerate for at least 2 hours to keep them moist. The taquitos may be refrigerated for up to 2 days before baking.
3. When ready to cook, preheat oven to 400°F. Lightly coat a sheet pan with cooking spray. Remove rolled taquitos from resealable bag one at a time. Place the taquitos seam side down on the pan and spray lightly with cooking spray. Bake for 20 minutes, until golden brown and crispy. Drain on paper towels.

Variation: For a lightly fried version, add 2 Tbsp peanut oil or canola oil to a heavy pot or deep skillet over medium-high heat. Using tongs, gently place 3–4 taquitos at a time in the hot oil, turning until golden brown and crispy, 2–3 minutes. Drain on paper towels. Repeat, using 2 Tbsp of oil at a time, for the remaining taquitos.

Note: There are many vegetarian meat fillers on the market. Find your favorite. I prefer the MorningStar Farms brand.

Veggie Taquitos

I love this taquito and often serve it as an appetizer: a crispy corn tortilla stuffed with fresh veggies.

1 cup shredded zucchini
1 cup shredded cabbage
1 medium-sized carrot, shredded
2 Tbsp minced onion
1/2 tsp salt
1/4 tsp black pepper
12 (6-inch) Fresh Corn Tortillas (page 72), micro-warmed (page 75)
Cooking spray

1. In a large bowl, combine zucchini, cabbage, carrot, and onion. Season with salt and pepper.
2. To build the taquitos, place 2 heaping Tbsp veggie mixture at one end of each tortilla. Gently roll the tortilla up and secure it with a toothpick. Place the rolled taquitos in a large resealable plastic bag to keep moist. Refrigerate until ready to cook or for up to 24 hours.
3. When ready to cook, preheat oven to 400°F. Lightly coat a sheet pan with cooking spray. Remove rolled taquitos from resealable bag one at a time. Place the taquitos seam side down on the pan and spray lightly with cooking spray. Bake for 20 minutes, turning twice, until golden brown and crispy. Drain on paper towels.

Variation: For a skillet-fried version, add 2 Tbsp oil to a deep skillet over medium-high heat. Using tongs, gently place 3–4 taquitos at a time in the hot oil, turning until golden brown and crispy, 2–3 minutes. Drain on paper towels. Repeat, using 2 Tbsp of oil at a time, for the remaining taquitos.

Serves: 12
Serving Size: 1 taquito
Prep Time: 15 minutes
Cook Time: 20 minutes

Choices/Exchanges
1 Starch

Basic Nutritional Values

Calories.................60
Calories from Fat..........5
Total Fat.................0.5 g
Saturated Fat...........0.1 g
Trans Fat...............0.0 g
Cholesterol.............0 mg
Sodium...............200 mg
Potassium............105 mg
Total Carbohydrate.......13 g
Dietary Fiber.............2 g
Sugars..................1 g
Protein.................2 g
Phosphorus...........40 mg

Sweet Potato Taquitos

Serves: 16
Serving Size: 1 taquito
Prep Time: 10 minutes
Cook Time: 30 minutes

Choices/Exchanges

1 Starch, 1/2 Fat

Basic Nutritional Values

Calories	110
Calories from Fat	25
Total Fat	3.0 g
Saturated Fat	1.4 g
Trans Fat	0.0 g
Cholesterol	10 mg
Sodium	240 mg
Potassium	180 mg
Total Carbohydrate	17 g
Dietary Fiber	2 g
Sugars	2 g
Protein	4 g
Phosphorus	105 mg

These taquitos have a sweet/savory flavor, heightened by the fresh cabbage and pungent cheese accents. Fill a platter with these taquitos—layered with freshness and flavor.

3 medium sweet potatoes
1/4 tsp salt
16 (6-inch) Fresh Corn Tortillas (page 72), micro-warmed (page 75)
2 cups shredded cabbage
1 cup crumbled cotija cheese

1. Poke the sweet potatoes with a fork, and microwave them on medium until tender (about 8-10 minutes). Remove, cool, and carefully peel. Place in a bowl, sprinkle with salt, and mash.
2. To build the taquitos, place 2 heaping Tbsp potatoes at one end of each tortilla. Gently roll tortilla up and secure it with a toothpick. Refrigerate until ready to cook, for up to 2 days.
3. When ready to cook, preheat oven to 400°F and spray a sheet pan with cooking spray. Remove rolled taquitos from resealable bag one at a time. Place the taquitos seam side down on the pan, and spray lightly with cooking spray. Bake for 20 minutes, turning twice, until golden brown and crispy. Drain on paper towels.
4. Place taquitos on individual serving plates and garnish with cabbage and cheese.

Variation: Moderation is key to maintaining good health. Still, I love to serve these deep-fried—once in a great while. To do this, first follow Steps 1 and 2. Instead of Step 3, fill a deep fryer, a deep heavy pot, or a deep skillet with 3 inches of oil, and heat to 350°F (measured on a candy thermometer). Using tongs, gently place 2-3 taquitos at a time in the hot oil and deep-fry, turning once, until crispy and golden brown, 2-3 minutes. Drain on paper towels. Follow Step 4.

Baked Chicken Flautas

Enjoy the crispy flaky texture these baked, chicken-stuffed flautas offer. These little hand-held gems are light and tasty.

2 cups Shredded Chicken (page 155)
1/2 tsp salt
8 (6-inch to 7-inch) low-carb whole-wheat flour tortillas, warmed (page 75)
Cooking spray
1 cup Tex-Mex Salsa (page 49)
1 cup Pickled Onions (page 55)

1. In a medium-sized bowl, combine chicken and salt.
2. To build the flautas, divide Shredded Chicken equally among tortillas, placing the chicken at one end of each tortilla. Gently roll tortilla up and secure with a toothpick. Place flautas in a resealable plastic bag to keep moist. Refrigerate to set for 1–2 hours or for up to 2 days.
3. When ready to cook flautas, preheat oven to 400°F. Spray a sheet pan with cooking spray. Remove flautas from resealable bag one at a time. Place flautas seam side down on the sheet pan and spray lightly with cooking spray. Bake for 20 minutes, turning twice, until golden brown and crispy. Serve with Tex-Mex Salsa and Pickled Onions.

Serves: 8
Serving Size: 1 flauta
Prep Time: 12 minutes
Chill Time: 1 hour
Cook Time: 20 minutes

Choices/Exchanges

1/2 Carbohydrate,
3 Lean Protein

Basic Nutritional Values

Calories	150
Calories from Fat	35
Total Fat	4.0 g
Saturated Fat	0.6 g
Trans Fat	0.0 g
Cholesterol	50 mg
Sodium	400 mg
Potassium	140 mg
Total Carbohydrate	10 g
Dietary Fiber	7 g
Sugars	0 g
Protein	23 g
Phosphorus	145 mg

Bean and Rice Flautas

Serves: 16
Serving Size: 1 flauta
Prep Time: 20 minutes
Cook Time: 20 minutes

Choices/Exchanges

2 Starch, 1 Lean Protein,
1/2 Fat

Basic Nutritional Values

Calories	210
Calories from Fat	50
Total Fat	6.0 g
Saturated Fat	0.9 g
Trans Fat	0.0 g
Cholesterol	0 mg
Sodium	290 mg
Potassium	270 mg
Total Carbohydrate	33 g
Dietary Fiber	5 g
Sugars	0 g
Protein	7 g
Phosphorus	145 mg

Crispy bean-filled flautas are the perfect vegetarian treat. Serve with Chile con Queso (page 35) or Classic Guacamole (page 29) for an appetizer.

> 2 cups Refried Beans (page 165) or store-bought reduced-fat refried beans in a brand of your choice
> 1 cup cooked brown or white rice
> 16 (8-inch) Fresh Whole-Grain Flour Tortillas (page 70), warmed (page 75)
> Cooking spray

1. In a medium-sized bowl, combine beans and rice, blending well.
2. To build the flautas, place 2 Tbsp of the bean mixture at one end of each tortilla. Gently roll the tortilla all the way up and secure with a toothpick. Repeat with remaining tortillas. Place rolled flautas in a resealable plastic bag to keep them moist and set. Refrigerate for up to 2 days. Bring to room temperature before cooking.
3. When ready to cook, preheat oven to 400°F. Lightly coat a sheet pan with cooking spray. Remove flautas from resealable bag one at a time. Place the flautas seam side down on the pan and spray lightly with cooking spray. Bake for 20 minutes, turning twice, until golden brown and crispy.

Tamales

Smoked Cheddar Cheese and Green Chile Tamales

Fresh chiles and a smoky cheese filling take these meatless tamales to a new level of flavor—rich and spicy.

> 2 cups shredded reduced-fat smoked cheddar cheese
> 1 cup chopped Roasted Green Chiles (page 152)
> 28 dried corn husks (see Tamale Preparation sidebar, page 134)
> 3 cups masa harina (see Tamale Preparation sidebar, page 134)
> 1 tsp baking powder
> 2 1/2 cups low-sodium chicken stock
> 1/2 cup shortening

1. In a medium-sized bowl, combine cheese and chiles until blended.
2. Submerge corn husks in water until soft and pliable, about 30 minutes. Remove from water, and dry on paper towels. Set up your assembly area with a cutting board, corn husks, a bowl of masa harina, and a bowl of cheese filling.
3. In a medium-sized bowl, combine masa and baking powder. Slowly add chicken stock and shortening. Knead by hand until well blended, 3–5 minutes. Masa should be pliable and moist, but firm. (If the masa is too stiff, add water, 1 Tbsp at a time.) Set aside.
4. Place damp corn husk on cutting board or work surface with the narrow end closest to you. Place another corn husk beside the first, overlapping along the long edges, with the wide end closest to you. Place 1/4 cup masa mixture in the center of overlapped husks. Using a spoon, spread masa into a rectangle about 1/4 inch thick over both corn husks.
5. Top masa with 1 Tbsp cheese filling, spreading filling down the center of the masa. Gently fold the right side of the corn husk toward the center, then toward the left side. Fold one end of the masa- and cheese-filled tamale toward the center.
6. Repeat with remaining corn husks.

Serves: 14
Serving Size: 1 tamale
Prep Time: 1 hour
Cook Time: 45 minutes

Choices/Exchanges
1 1/2 Starch,
1 Lean Protein, 1 1/2 Fat

Basic Nutritional Values

Calories	220
Calories from Fat	110
Total Fat	12.0 g
Saturated Fat	4.0 g
Trans Fat	0.0 g
Cholesterol	10 mg
Sodium	180 mg
Potassium	190 mg
Total Carbohydrate	21 g
Dietary Fiber	3 g
Sugars	0 g
Protein	8 g
Phosphorus	205 mg

7. In a large pot, over medium-high heat, boil about 2 inches water. Place the steam insert in the pot. Place tamales in the pot with the folded end down, making sure that the tamales are not touching. Cover and steam until dough around the filling is firm, 45 minutes to 1 hour. To check for doneness: The masa should pull away easily from the corn husks, should be firm, and should encase the filling.

TAMALE PREPARATION

1. You will need a large pot with a steam insert and a lid.
2. You can purchase a 16-oz bag of dried corn husks online or in the ethnic foods section of your local grocery store.
3. Buy masa harina in the ethnic foods or Mexican food section of your grocery store or online. You can add spices such as red chili powder or garlic powder to your masa. If the masa is too sticky, use a corn husk or large flat spoon to press it into place.

Spinach Asparagus Tamales

This light vegetable filling adds depth and freshness. Rich asparagus and spinach teamed with a touch of creamy cheese are a tasty combination.

2 cups chopped cooked asparagus
1/2 cup chopped cooked spinach
1 cup (about 4 oz) shredded reduced-fat Monterey Jack cheese
28 dried corn husks (see Tamale Preparation sidebar, page 134)
3 cups masa harina (see Tamale Preparation sidebar, page 134)
1 tsp baking powder
2 1/2 cups reduced-sodium chicken stock
1/2 cup shortening

1. In a medium-sized bowl, combine asparagus, spinach, and cheese until blended.
2. Submerge corn husks in water until soft and pliable, about 30 minutes. Remove from water and dry on paper towels. Set up your assembly area with a cutting board, corn husks, bowl of masa harina, and bowl of vegetable filling.
3. In a medium-sized bowl, combine masa and baking powder. Slowly add chicken stock and shortening. Knead by hand until well blended, 3–5 minutes. Masa should be pliable and moist but firm. (If the masa is too stiff, add water, 1 Tbsp at a time.) Set aside.
4. Place damp corn husk on cutting board or work surface with the narrow end closest to you. Place another corn husk beside the first, overlapping along the long edges, with the wide end closest to you. Place 1/4 cup masa mixture in the center of overlapped husks. Using a spoon, spread masa into a rectangle about 1/4 inch thick over both corn husks.
5. Top masa with 1 Tbsp vegetable filling, spreading filling down the center of the masa. Gently fold the right side of the corn husk toward the center, then toward the left side. Fold one end of the masa- and veggie/cheese-filled tamale toward the center.
6. Repeat with remaining corn husks.
7. In a large pot over medium-high heat, boil about 2 inches water. Place the steam insert in the pot. Place tamales in the pot with the folded end down, making sure that the tamales are not touching. Cover and steam until dough is firm around the vegetable filling, 45 minutes to 1 hour. To check for doneness: The masa should pull away easily from the corn husks, and it should be firm and encase the filling.

Serves: 14
Serving Size: 1 tamale
Prep Time: 1 hour
Cook Time: 45 minutes

Choices/Exchanges
1 1/2 Starch,
1 Lean Protein, 1 Fat

Basic Nutritional Values

Calories	200
Calories from Fat	90
Total Fat	10.0 g
Saturated Fat	3.0 g
Trans Fat	0.0 g
Cholesterol	5 mg
Sodium	130 mg
Potassium	200 mg
Total Carbohydrate	22 g
Dietary Fiber	3 g
Sugars	0 g
Protein	6 g
Phosphorus	160 mg

Red Chile Tamales

This Mexican tradition is typically shared around the Christmas holidays. Making these tamales is a true labor of love. Prepare the meat filling in advance to cut down on the assembly time.

28 dried corn husks (see Tamale Preparation sidebar, page 134)
3 cups masa harina (see Tamale Preparation sidebar, page 134)
1 tsp baking powder
2 1/2 cups reduced-sodium chicken stock
1/2 cup shortening
14 Tbsp Red Chile Pork (page 154)

1. Submerge corn husks in water until soft and pliable, about 30 minutes. Remove from water and dry on paper towels. Set up your assembly area with a cutting board, corn husks, a bowl of masa harina, and a bowl of meat filling.
2. In a medium-sized bowl, combine masa and baking powder. Slowly add chicken stock and shortening. Knead by hand until well blended, 3–5 minutes. Masa should be pliable and moist but firm. (If the masa is too stiff, add water, 1 Tbsp at a time.) Set aside.
3. Place damp corn husk on cutting board or work surface with the narrow end closest to you Place another corn husk beside the first, overlapping along the long edges, with the wide end closest to you. Place 1/4 cup masa mixture in the center of overlapped husks. Using a spoon, spread masa into a rectangle about 1/4 inch thick over both corn husks.
4. Top masa with 1 Tbsp Red Chile Pork filling, spreading filling down the center of the masa. Gently fold the right side of the corn husk toward the center, then toward the left side. Fold one end of the masa- and meat-filled tamale toward the center.
5. Repeat with remaining corn husks.
6. In a large pot over medium-high heat, boil about 2 inches water. Place the steam insert in the pot. Place tamales in the pot with the folded end down, making sure that the tamales are not touching. Cover and steam until dough is firm around the meat filling, 45 minutes to 1 hour. To check for doneness, the masa should pull away easily from the corn husks and should be firm and encase the filling.

Serves: 14
Serving Size: 1 tamale
Prep Time: 1 hour
Cook Time: 45 minutes

Choices/Exchanges
1 1/2 Starch, 2 Fat

Basic Nutritional Values

Calories	200
Calories from Fat	100
Total Fat	.0 g
Saturated Fat	2.6 g
Trans Fat	0.0 g
Cholesterol	10 mg
Sodium	85 mg
Potassium	170 mg
Total Carbohydrate	21 g
Dietary Fiber	3 g
Sugars	0 g
Protein	6 g
Phosphorus	130 mg

Burritos

Basic Nutritional Values

Calories	560
Calories from Fat	140
Total Fat	16.0 g
Saturated Fat	5.5 g
Trans Fat	0.0 g
Cholesterol	115 mg
Sodium	600 mg
Potassium	1290 mg
Total Carbohydrate	51 g
Dietary Fiber	9 g
Sugars	7 g
Protein	54 g
Phosphorus	595 mg

Fiber-Full Burrito Bowls

These bowls are great for low-carb eaters! Start with rice on the bottom, then a protein filling, then your favorite garnishes. I like to offer a variety of these: diced tomato, chopped cilantro, Pickled Onions (page 55), 1 oz of your favorite shredded cheese—the possibilities are endless!

2 cups Mexican Rice (page 168), warmed
2 cups Shredded Chicken (page 155), warmed, or Tex-Mex Shrimp (page 156)
1 cup Pinto Beans (page 164), warmed
1 cup (about 4 oz) shredded reduced-fat Monterey Jack cheese or cheddar cheese
1/4 cup Classic Guacamole (page 29) or a store-bought brand of your choice
2 cups diced tomatoes
4 cups mixed salad greens
1/2 cup Pico de Gallo (page 48)

1. Divide rice equally into 4 serving bowls. Top with equal amounts of chicken or shrimp. Then add equal amounts of beans.
2. Garnish with equal amounts of cheese, guacamole, tomatoes, salad greens, and Pico de Gallo. Serve immediately.

Variations: Create your own winning combination.

Machaca Burritos

This beefy filling is infused with a citrusy chile flavor. The word *machaca* comes from the Spanish verb *machacar*, meaning "to pound or crush." Historically, this meat was seasoned, cured, and dried for many hours. Today, you can make it just as tasty by infusing flavor and cooking out the juices. I like to serve Machaca Burritos enchilada-style with a sauce such as Tex-Mex Chile Gravy (page 61).

1 Tbsp vegetable oil
2 cloves garlic, minced
1 medium onion, diced
1/2 cup Roasted Green Chiles (page 152)
1 medium tomato, seeded and chopped
2 cups Shredded Beef (page 153)
1/3 cup unsalted beef stock
Juice of 1 lime
Juice of 1 lemon
1/4 tsp black pepper
4 (10-inch) Fresh Whole-Grain Flour Tortillas (page 71), warmed (page 75)
1 cup Tex-Mex Chile Gravy (page 61) (see Note)
1/2 cup (about 4 oz) shredded reduced-fat cheddar cheese
4 cups shredded lettuce

1. Preheat oven to 375°F.
2. In a large skillet, heat oil over medium-low heat. Add garlic, onion, chiles, and tomato. Cook, stirring, until onion is translucent, 8–10 minutes. Add beef, beef stock, and juices. Increase heat to medium and cook, stirring, until all juices have evaporated, 12–15 minutes. Season with pepper.
3. To build the burritos, divide meat mixture equally at the bottom edge of each tortilla. Fold bottom edge of tortilla up over filling. Starting at folded bottom edge, roll up to enclose filling. Secure with a toothpick. Repeat with remaining tortillas.
4. Place each burrito on an individual ovenproof plate, seam side down. Divide gravy and cheese equally among burritos. Bake until cheese is melted and burritos are heated through, 12–15 minutes. Garnish each with lettuce.

Note: For something different, crown this burrito with different sauces. In place of the Tex-Mex Chile Gravy, substitute 2 cups Red Enchilada Sauce (page 63), which has a rich earthy flavor, or 2 cups Green Enchilada Sauce (page 64), which adds a lighter, spicy flavor.

Serves: 4
Serving Size: 1 burrito
Prep Time: 20 minutes
Cook Time: 40 minutes

Choices/Exchanges

2 1/2 Starch, 2 Nonstarchy Vegetable, 4 Lean Protein, 4 Fat

Basic Nutritional Values

Calories	620
Calories from Fat	270
Total Fat	30.0 g
Saturated Fat	6.5 g
Trans Fat	0.4 g
Cholesterol	115 mg
Sodium	700 mg
Potassium	1040 mg
Total Carbohydrate	47 g
Dietary Fiber	9 g
Sugars	5 g
Protein	47 g
Phosphorus	570 mg

Chile Verde Burritos, p. 141; Michelada, p. 13

Chile Verde Burritos

These burritos are so satisfying and low in fat and calories. Make the chicken filling ahead for quick, easy meal prep.

1/4 cup chicken stock, divided use
1 clove garlic, minced
1/2 cup Roasted Green Chiles (page 152)
1 medium onion, diced
2 cups diced, cooked chicken or Shredded Chicken (page 155)
4 (10-inch) Fresh Whole-Grain Flour Tortillas (page 71), warmed (page 75)
1 cup Green Chile Enchilada Sauce (page 64)
1 cup (about 4 oz) shredded reduced-fat Monterey Jack cheese
2 cups diced tomatoes
4 cups shredded lettuce

1. Preheat oven to 375°F.
2. Coat a large skillet lightly with cooking spray. Over medium heat, add 2 Tbsp chicken stock, garlic, chiles, and onion. Cook, stirring, until onion is translucent, 4–6 minutes. Add chicken and remaining stock. Simmer, stirring occasionally, until chicken is heated through, about 8–10 minutes.
3. To build the burritos, divide chicken mixture equally at bottom edge of each tortilla. Fold bottom edge of tortilla up over filling. Starting at folded bottom edge, roll up to enclose filling. Secure with a toothpick. Repeat with remaining tortillas.
4. Place each burrito on an ovenproof plate, seam side down. Pour 1/4 cup sauce over each burrito, and top with cheese. Bake until cheese is melted and burrito is heated through, 12–15 minutes. Garnish with tomatoes and shredded lettuce.

Serves: 4
Serving Size: 1 burrito
Prep Time: 20 minutes
Cook Time: About 30 minutes

Choices/Exchanges

2 Starch, 3 Nonstarchy Vegetable, 4 Lean Protein, 3 Fat

Basic Nutritional Values

Calories	530
Calories from Fat	210
Total Fat	23.0 g
Saturated Fat	6.1 g
Trans Fat	0.0 g
Cholesterol	85 mg
Sodium	490 mg
Potassium	1010 mg
Total Carbohydrate	48 g
Dietary Fiber	9 g
Sugars	7 g
Protein	37 g
Phosphorus	520 mg

Bean and Cheese Chimichangas

Serves: 4
Serving Size: 1 chimichanga
Prep Time: 10 minutes
Chill Time: 1 hour
Cook Time: 12 minutes

Choices/Exchanges

4 Starch, 2 Nonstarchy Vegetable, 1 Lean Protein, 3 Fat

Basic Nutritional Values

Calories	540
Calories from Fat	180
Total Fat	20.0 g
Saturated Fat	6.2 g
Trans Fat	0.0 g
Cholesterol	25 mg
Sodium	600 mg
Potassium	1210 mg
Total Carbohydrate	72 g
Dietary Fiber	15 g
Sugars	6 g
Protein	25 g
Phosphorus	525 mg

Historically, chimichangas are burritos filled with a savory filling, deep-fried until golden brown, smothered in a mild enchilada sauce, and covered in melted cheese. However, to reduce fat I bake them at a high temperature until golden brown. They're a great hand-held food when you're on the go.

> 2 cups Refried Beans (page 165) or store-bought reduced-fat refried beans in a brand of your choice
> 4 (10-inch) Fresh Whole-Grain Flour Tortillas (page 71), warmed (page 75)
> 1 cup (about 4 oz) shredded reduced-fat Monterey Jack cheese
> Cooking spray
> 4 cups shredded lettuce
> 2 1/2 cups diced tomatoes

1. Preheat to 400°F.
2. To build the chimichangas, place 1/2 cup beans on bottom half of each tortilla. Sprinkle with cheese, dividing equally. Fold bottom edge of tortilla up over the beans. Fold in both sides of tortilla. Starting at folded bottom edge, roll up to enclose filling. Secure with a toothpick.
3. Place chimichangas in a resealable plastic bag to set and keep moist. Refrigerate sealed bag for at least 1 hour to firm up filling, or for up to 4 hours.
4. When ready to cook, lightly coat each filled tortilla with cooking spray. Place seam side down on baking sheet. Bake for 6–8 minutes, then turn over and bake for 6 minutes more, until golden brown.
5. Remove from baking sheet. Place each chimichanga on individual plates and garnish with lettuce and tomatoes.

Variation: To serve enchilada-style, after baking the chimichangas, divide 2 cups Green Enchilada Sauce (page 64), warmed, and 1 cup shredded reduced-fat cheese evenly over each chimichanga. Serve immediately. For a hand-held chimichanga, wrap in a napkin and eat immediately.

Enchiladas

Cheesy Green Chile Enchiladas

Enchiladas are great for a crowd or as a "make ahead" entrée. These corn tortillas filled with tender chicken or shrimp are tasty and healthy.

2 cloves garlic, minced
1/4 cup chicken broth
1/2 cup Roasted Green Chiles (page 152)
1 medium onion, minced
3 cups cooked, cubed chicken or Shredded Chicken (page 155)
12 (6-inch) Fresh Corn Tortillas (page 72), micro-warmed (page 75)
2 cups Green Enchilada Sauce (page 64) or store-bought in a brand of your choice
1 cup (about 4 oz) shredded reduced-fat cheddar cheese
1 cup (about 4 oz) shredded reduced-fat Monterey Jack cheese

1. Preheat oven to 350°F.
2. Coat a large skillet lightly with cooking spray. Add garlic and chicken broth and cook over medium heat until tender, about 1 minute. Add chiles and onion, cooking and stirring until onion is translucent, about 3–5 minutes. Add chicken and simmer until chicken is heated through, 2–3 minutes.
3. Coat a 13 x 9-inch glass baking dish lightly with cooking spray. Place 1/4 cup chicken mixture at end of each tortilla. Roll up tortilla and place seam side down in baking dish. Repeat with remaining tortillas.
4. Spray rolled enchiladas with cooking spray. Top rolled enchiladas with Green Enchilada Sauce and cheeses.
5. Bake until enchiladas are heated through and cheese is melted, about 20–25 minutes.

Variations:
- For Green Chile Shrimp Enchiladas, substitute 3 cups of shrimp—cooked, peeled, deveined, and chopped—for the chicken in Step 2. Follow Steps 3–5.
- For Green Chile Vegetarian Enchiladas, omit garlic, chicken broth, and chicken. Substitute 3 cups Zucchini and Corn Medley (page 162), and heat as in Step 2. Follow Steps 3–5.

Serves: 12
Serving Size: 1 enchilada
Prep Time: 20 minutes
Cook Time: 35 minutes

Choices/Exchanges

1 Starch, 2 Lean Protein, 1 Fat

Basic Nutritional Values

Calories. 220
Calories from Fat 90
Total Fat . . . . .10.0 g
Saturated Fat . . . . .3.5 g
Trans Fat . . . . .0.0 g
Cholesterol . . . . 45 mg
Sodium . . . . 310 mg
Potassium . . . . 320 mg
Total Carbohydrate. . . . . . . .17 g
Dietary Fiber . . . . 3 g
Sugars. . . . . .1 g
Protein . . . . .17 g
Phosphorus . . . . 235 mg

Tex-Mex Cheese Enchiladas, p. 145; Zucchini and Corn Medley (Calabacitas), p. 162

Tex-Mex Cheese Enchiladas

Texas true . . . these are the cheesy Tex-Mex enchiladas that got their start in the 1920s. Thoughtfully selected cheeses and cooking techniques help cut the calories. Serve as a main dish or a side dish.

3 cups (about 12 oz) shredded 50% reduced-fat sharp cheddar cheese (such as Cabot), divided use
12 (6-inch) Fresh Corn Tortillas (page 72), micro-warmed (page 75)
1 1/2 cups Tex-Mex Chile Gravy (page 61)
1 cup (about 4 oz) shredded reduced-fat Monterey Jack cheese
1 cup fat-free sour cream
4 green onions, mostly green part, minced
1/2 cup sliced black olives

1. Preheat oven to 350°F and lightly coat a 13 x 9-inch glass baking dish with cooking spray.
2. Place 1/4 cup cheddar cheese at end of a tortilla. Roll up tortilla and place seam side down in a baking dish. Repeat with remaining tortillas.
3. Spray rolled enchiladas with cooking spray, and top evenly with gravy and Monterey Jack cheese.
4. Bake until enchiladas are heated through and cheese is melted, about 20–25 minutes. Serve garnished equally with sour cream, onions, and olives.

Serves: 12
Serving Size: 1 enchilada
Prep Time: 30 minutes
Cook Time: 25 minutes

Choices/Exchanges

1 Starch, 2 Medium-Fat Protein

Basic Nutritional Values

Calories	220
Calories from Fat	100
Total Fat	11.0 g
Saturated Fat	4.9 g
Trans Fat	0.0 g
Cholesterol	25 mg
Sodium	470 mg
Potassium	170 mg
Total Carbohydrate	19 g
Dietary Fiber	2 g
Sugars	1 g
Protein	14 g
Phosphorus	255 mg

Sour Cream Green Chile Enchiladas

Serves: 10
Serving Size: 1 enchilada
Prep Time: 20 minutes
Cook Time: 30 minutes

Choices/Exchanges

1 Starch, 1/2 Carbohydrate,
3 Lean Protein, 1/2 Fat

Basic Nutritional Values

Calories	280
Calories from Fat	80
Total Fat	9.0 g
Saturated Fat	2.8 g
Trans Fat	0.0 g
Cholesterol	50 mg
Sodium	470 mg
Potassium	470 mg
Total Carbohydrate	26 g
Dietary Fiber	3 g
Sugars	2 g
Protein	24 g
Phosphorus	285 mg

This is a rich, flavorful enchilada. Fat-free sour cream cuts the calories and makes this a healthy indulgence.

2 Tbsp reduced-sodium chicken stock
2 cloves garlic, minced
1 1/2 cups Roasted Green Chiles (page 152)
2 cups Shredded Chicken (page 155)
1 cup fat-free sour cream
1 (10.75-oz) can reduced-fat condensed cream of chicken soup
1/2 tsp ground black pepper
Cooking spray
10 (8-inch) Fresh Whole-Grain Flour Tortillas (page 70), warmed (page 75)
1 1/2 cups (about 6 oz) shredded 50% reduced-fat sharp cheddar cheese (such as Cabot)
4 green onions, green part only, minced

1. Preheat oven to 350°F.
2. In a large skillet over medium heat, combine chicken stock, garlic, and green chiles. Cook, stirring, for 1 minute. Add chicken and cook until heated through, 2–3 minutes. Set aside.
3. In a large bowl, whisk together sour cream and condensed soup. Reserve 3/4 cup mixture for topping. Add chicken mixture to remaining sour cream mixture and mix well. Blend in pepper.
4. To build the enchiladas, coat a 13 x 9-inch glass baking dish lightly with cooking spray. Divide chicken mixture at end of each tortilla. Roll up tortilla, and place seam side down in baking dish.
5. Lightly coat the ends of each rolled tortilla with cooking spray. Top the enchiladas evenly with remaining sour cream mixture and cheese.
6. Bake until tortillas are golden brown on the edges, cheese is melted and heated through, 25–30 minutes. Garnish with onions and serve immediately.

Tip

For a weeknight time-saver, make these enchiladas a day ahead. Just follow Steps 1–5, then cover and refrigerate overnight. When ready to serve, remove from refrigerator and let stand at room temperature for up to 15 minutes, then follow Step 6.

Red Chile Beefy Street Enchiladas

Fresh Corn Tortillas stuffed with a beefy filling and smothered in a chile sauce melt in your mouth. I often set out small bowls of sliced olives, minced green onions, sour cream, diced tomato, chopped cilantro, and shredded iceberg lettuce as garnish. In certain areas of the Southwest, it's popular to add toasted pecan pieces to red and green enchiladas for even more texture and flavor. Find your favorite!

- 1 1/2 lb 93% lean ground beef, cooked and crumbled
- 1/8 tsp salt
- 1/4 tsp pepper
- 12 (6-inch) Fresh Corn Tortillas (page 72), micro-warmed (page 75)
- 2 cups Red Enchilada Sauce (page 63) or a store-bought brand of your choice
- 1 cup (about 4 oz) shredded reduced-fat cheddar cheese
- 1 cup (about 4 oz) shredded reduced-fat Monterey Jack cheese
- 1/2 cup sliced black olives
- 4 green onions, green part only, chopped

1. Preheat oven to 350°F.
2. In a medium-sized skillet, season the meat with salt and pepper, then cook until browned and cooked through. Drain excess fat.
3. Place 1/4 cup ground beef at end of each tortilla. Roll up tortilla, and place seam side down in prepared baking dish. Repeat with remaining tortillas. Lightly coat rolled enchiladas with cooking spray, and top with sauce and cheeses.
4. Bake until enchiladas are heated through and cheese is melted, about 20–25 minutes. Allow enchiladas to cool 5 minutes then garnish with olives and onions.

Variations:
- For Red Enchiladas with Shredded Beef, substitute 3 cups Shredded Beef (page 153) for the ground beef. Continue with Step 3.
- For Green Chile Vegetarian Enchiladas, substitute 3 cups Zucchini and Corn Medley (page 162), warmed, for the ground beef. Continue with Step 3.

Serves: 12
Serving Size: 1 enchilada
Prep Time: 20 minutes
Cook Time: 25 minutes

Choices/Exchanges

1 Starch, 2 Lean Protein, 2 Fat

Basic Nutritional Values

Calories	250
Calories from Fat	130
Total Fat	14.0 g
Saturated Fat	4.7 g
Trans Fat	0.2 g
Cholesterol	45 mg
Sodium	480 mg
Potassium	310 mg
Total Carbohydrate	16 g
Dietary Fiber	3 g
Sugars	2 g
Protein	18 g
Phosphorus	240 mg

Stacked Saucy Enchiladas with Fresh Greens

Serves: 6
Serving Size: 1 (2-tortilla) stack
Prep Time: 12 minutes
Cook Time: 14 minutes

Choices/Exchanges

1 1/2 Starch, 1 Nonstarchy Vegetable, 1 Lean Protein, 1 1/2 Fat

Basic Nutritional Values

Calories	240
Calories from Fat	90
Total Fat	10.0 g
Saturated Fat	3.2 g
Trans Fat	0.0 g
Cholesterol	10 mg
Sodium	490 mg
Potassium	340 mg
Total Carbohydrate	32 g
Dietary Fiber	6 g
Sugars	3 g
Protein	9 g
Phosphorus	210 mg

This is a favorite weeknight meal—quick and easy! Sauce it, stack it, place it in the oven to melt, and it's done. Yet another way to serve the traditional enchilada.

1 cup Red Enchilada Sauce (page 63) or a store-bought brand of your choice
12 (6-inch) Fresh Corn Tortillas (page 72), micro-warmed (page 75)
1 cup minced onion
1 cup (about 4 oz) shredded reduced-fat cheddar cheese
6 cups chopped mixed lettuce greens
6 radishes, thinly sliced

1. Preheat oven to 375°F.
2. In a medium-sized skillet over low heat, warm enchilada sauce. Using tongs, dip tortillas, one at a time, in sauce, allowing excess sauce to drip off into the pan.
3. Place sauce-coated tortillas on individual ovenproof plates. Top each tortilla with about 1 Tbsp onion and 1 Tbsp cheese, spreading to the edges. Repeat with remaining tortillas and onions, so there are two layers on each plate. Top with remaining cheese.
4. Bake until cheese is completely melted and tortillas are heated through, 8–10 minutes.
5. Garnish each plate with greens (1 cup per stack) and radishes.

Variation: For Tex-Mex Stacked Breakfast Enchiladas, after baking or microwaving the enchiladas, top each stack with an egg, cooked to order. Omit the lettuce and the cheese.

Tip

You can also microwave each plate on medium-high (70%) power in 1-minute intervals until heated through.

And More

Torta de Fresco (Mexican Sandwich)

This Mexican sandwich is piled high with tender meat and crowned with spice! A low-carb roll and reduced-fat cheese keep it light.

1 cup Shredded Beef (page 153)
4 whole-wheat sandwich thin rolls, split
1 avocado, seeded and mashed
1/2 cup (about 2 oz) shredded reduced-fat Monterey Jack cheese
1 cup Pico de Gallo (page 48)
1 1/2 cups chopped mixed lettuce greens
12 slices pickled jalapeño peppers

1. In a skillet, heat beef over medium heat and season with salt and pepper to taste (if desired), stirring often, until meat is heated through. Remove from heat.
2. Lightly toast both halves of each roll. Spread cut side of top half with mashed avocado. Top each bottom half with equal amounts of beef, cheese, Pico de Gallo, and greens. Garnish with slices of jalapeño, and cover with top half of roll.

Variation: Use Shredded Chicken (page 155) instead of beef.

Serves: 4
Serving Size: 1 sandwich
Prep Time: 20 minutes
Cook Time: About 5 minutes

Choices/Exchanges

1 1/2 Starch, 1 Nonstarchy Vegetable, 3 Lean Protein, 1 Fat

Basic Nutritional Values

Calories. 330
 Calories from Fat 110
Total Fat . . . . .12.0 g
 Saturated Fat . . . . .3.1 g
 Trans Fat . . . . .0.0 g
Cholesterol . . . . 60 mg
Sodium . . . . 420 mg
Potassium . . . . 730 mg
Total Carbohydrate. . . . . . . .31 g
 Dietary Fiber . . . . 10 g
 Sugars. . . . . .7 g
Protein . . . . 29 g
Phosphorus . . . . 310 mg

Baked Chile Rellenos

Serves: 9
Serving Size: 1 rectangular
piece (4 1/3 x 3 inches)
Prep Time: 15 minutes
Cook Time: 45 minutes

Choices/Exchanges

1 Carbohydrate, 2 Lean
Protein, 1 Fat

Basic Nutritional Values

Calories	200
Calories from Fat	90
Total Fat	10.0 g
Saturated Fat	5.0 g
Trans Fat	0.0 g
Cholesterol	185 mg
Sodium	330 mg
Potassium	420 mg
Total Carbohydrate	11 g
Dietary Fiber	1 g
Sugars	3 g
Protein	16 g
Phosphorus	335 mg

This casserole-style dish is so versatile. It can be served as a side dish or a main dish, for breakfast, lunch, or dinner. It is the essence of the chile relleno (pronounced *ray-eh-no*): spicy green chiles and rich creamy cheeses held together with a delicate egg batter.

1/2 cup all-purpose flour
1/2 tsp baking powder
8 large eggs
2 egg whites
1 cup skim milk
1 1/2 cups (about 6 oz) shredded 50% reduced-fat sharp cheddar cheese (such as Cabot)
1 cup (about 4 oz) shredded reduced-fat Monterey Jack cheese
3 cups chopped Roasted Green Chiles (page 152)

1. Preheat oven to 350°F.
2. In a medium-sized bowl, combine flour and baking powder.
3. In a separate medium-sized bowl, using an electric mixer, beat eggs and egg whites until light and fluffy, 2–3 minutes. Add milk and blend well. Slowly mix in dry ingredients.
4. Fold in cheeses.
5. Coat a 13 x 9-inch glass baking dish lightly with cooking spray. Arrange chiles over the bottom of the baking dish. Pour egg mixture equally over chiles.
6. Bake until center is firm and edges are slightly browned, 35–45 minutes. Let stand for 5 minutes before serving.

Savory Stuffed Sopapillas

Enjoy a savory filling in these heavenly pastry pockets. Sopapillas puffed up without frying are perfect for meat, cheeses, and fresh garnishes.

4 Light Sopapillas (page 72), warmed
2 cups Tex-Mex Chile con Carne (page 99), warmed
1 cup (about 4 oz) shredded reduced-fat Monterey Jack cheese
1 cup shredded iceberg lettuce
1 tomato, seeded and diced
1 medium onion, minced

1. Slice open each sopapilla at one end. Divide Tex-Mex Chile con Carne equally and spoon into sopapillas.
2. Stuff filled sopapillas with equal amounts of cheese, lettuce, tomato, and onion.
3. Serve immediately.

Serves: 4
Serving Size: 1 stuffed
  sopapilla
Prep Time: 12 minutes
Cook Time: N/A

Choices/Exchanges

1 Starch, 1 Nonstarchy
Vegetable, 2 Lean Protein,
1 Fat

Basic Nutritional Values

Calories. 240
  Calories from Fat 80
Total Fat . . . . .9.0 g
  Saturated Fat . . . . .4.3 g
  Trans Fat . . . . .0.1 g
Cholesterol . . . . 45 mg
Sodium . . . . 430 mg
Potassium . . . . 460 mg
Total Carbohydrate. . . . . . . 22 g
  Dietary Fiber . . . . 4 g
  Sugars. . . . . 4 g
Protein . . . . 19 g
Phosphorus . . . . 345 mg

ROASTED GREEN CHILES

To roast chiles, such as Anaheim, poblano, and jalapeño:

1. Preheat oven broiler to high.
2. Arrange fresh chiles on a baking sheet and place under the broiler, 2–3 inches away from the heat.
3. Broil, turning often with tongs, until surfaces of skin are lightly charred and blistered.
4. Immediately place chiles in a paper or plastic bag or an airtight container, and close tightly. Let chiles cool for 12–15 minutes.
5. Remove from bag, peel away charred skin, and remove stems and seeds. Tear into strips or chop, as needed.
6. Refrigerate chiles for up to 3 days, or freeze in an airtight container for up to 6 months.

Note: Yields for chopped medium-sized green chiles: 2 chiles = 1/4 cup, 4 chiles = 1/2 cup, and 8 chiles = 1 cup.

Outdoor Chile Roasting

To roast chiles, such as Anaheim, poblano, and jalapeño:

1. Preheat greased barbecue grill to medium.
2. Arrange fresh chiles on the grill rack.
3. Grill, turning often with tongs, until surfaces of skin are lightly charred and blistered.
4. Immediately place chiles in a paper or plastic bag or an airtight container, and close tightly. Let chiles cool for 12–15 minutes.
5. Remove from bag, peel away charred skin, and remove stems and seeds. Tear into strips or chop, as needed.
6. Refrigerate chiles for up to 3 days, or freeze in an airtight container for up to 6 months.

SHREDDED BEEF

Slow-cooked beef creates a perfect shredded filling for Tex-Mex cooking. After it's slow-cooked, the beef should be falling apart and easy to shred. Measure out what you need for each recipe, and freeze the remaining meat in an airtight container for up to 3 months.

3 lb lean (no visible fat) boneless beef chuck or sirloin roast
3 cloves garlic
3/4 tsp salt

Serves: 8
Serving Size: 1/2 cup
Prep Time: 10 minutes
Cook Time: 2 hours

Choices/Exchanges

5 Lean Protein

Basic Nutritional Values

Calories	210
Calories from Fat	70
Total Fat	8.0 g
Saturated Fat	2.8 g
Trans Fat	0.3 g
Cholesterol	105 mg
Sodium	280 mg
Potassium	390 mg
Total Carbohydrate	0 g
Dietary Fiber	0 g
Sugars	0 g
Protein	34 g
Phosphorus	255 mg

1. Place roast in a large pot, and fill with enough water to cover the meat by 2 inches. Add garlic, and bring to a gentle boil over medium-high heat.
2. Cover, reduce heat to medium-low, and simmer until meat is tender and falling apart, 1 1/2–2 hours.
3. Remove meat from pot. Discard broth.
4. Transfer meat to a cutting board, and let cool to room temperature. Shred meat into strands with your fingers or with two forks. Add salt and mix well. Let cool completely.
5. Measure out amount needed for recipe. Place remaining beef in a resealable plastic bag, and refrigerate for up to 2 days or freeze for up to 3 months.

Slow-Cooker Method: Add roast, garlic, and 1 cup water to slow-cooker stoneware. Slow-cook on high for 4–5 hours. Strain, discarding broth and garlic. Transfer meat to a cutting board, and let cool to room temperature. Shred meat into strands with your fingers or with two forks. Add salt and mix well. Let cool completely. Follow Step 5.

RED CHILE PORK

This pork filling in a thick red chile sauce can be used in many Tex-Mex dishes. Top a tostada, fill a burrito, or fold into a taco. It's a meal in itself!

2 lb boneless pork shoulder blade (butt), fat trimmed, cut into bite-size pieces
2 cups Red Enchilada Sauce (page 63)
1 tsp crushed red pepper flakes
1 tsp dried Mexican oregano
1 tsp ground cumin
1 tsp garlic powder
1 tsp onion powder

Serves: 8
Serving Size: 1/2 cup
Prep Time: 10 minutes
Cook Time: 1 hour

Choices/Exchanges

1 Nonstarchy Vegetable,
3 Medium-Fat Protein,
1 Fat

Basic Nutritional Values

Calories	290
Calories from Fat	170
Total Fat	19.0 g
Saturated Fat	5.2 g
Trans Fat	0.0 g
Cholesterol	80 mg
Sodium	270 mg
Potassium	420 mg
Total Carbohydrate	6 g
Dietary Fiber	2 g
Sugars	2 g
Protein	23 g
Phosphorus	215 mg

1. Place pork in a large pot, and add just enough water to cover the meat. Bring to a boil over medium-high heat for 6–8 minutes.
2. Reduce heat and boil gently, stirring occasionally, until water and juices have evaporated, 30–40 minutes.
3. Reduce heat to low. Add Red Enchilada Sauce and spices. Mix well over medium-low heat, until spices are well blended and sauce is heated through.

SHREDDED CHICKEN

Chicken is a great filling in Tex-Mex cuisine. For a quick go-to filling, I keep a container of it in the refrigerator or the freezer most of the time.

1 1/2 lb boneless, skinless chicken breasts
3 cloves garlic

1. Place chicken in a large pot and fill with enough water to cover the chicken by about 2 inches. Add garlic, and bring to a gentle boil over medium-high heat.
2. Reduce heat to medium-low and simmer gently until chicken is tender and no longer pink inside, about 20 minutes.
3. Remove chicken from pot. Discard broth and garlic.
4. Transfer chicken to a cutting board. Let chicken cool to room temperature. Shred chicken with your fingers or with two forks.
5. Measure out amount needed for recipe. Place remaining chicken in a resealable plastic bag, and refrigerate for up to 2 days or freeze for up to 4 months.

Serves: 4
Serving Size: 1/2 cup
Prep Time: 10 minutes
Cook Time: 20 minutes

Choices/Exchanges

5 Lean Protein

Basic Nutritional Values

Calories	190
Calories from Fat	35
Total Fat	4.0 g
Saturated Fat	1.1 g
Trans Fat	0.0 g
Cholesterol	95 mg
Sodium	80 mg
Potassium	240 mg
Total Carbohydrate	0 g
Dietary Fiber	0 g
Sugars	0 g
Protein	37 g
Phosphorus	210 mg

Tips
- To reheat chicken, place desired amount in a microwave-safe bowl. Cover and microwave on high for 1 minute. Remove and stir. Repeat until chicken is completely warmed through, 2–3 minutes.
- Chicken breasts are generally 5 oz each. At this size, once a breast is cooked and shredded, it yields about 1/2 cup cooked chicken.

TEX-MEX SHRIMP

Grilled or broiled shrimp—so simple to prepare—can be used in so many Tex-Mex recipes. Lots of spice gives this shrimp a distinctive flavor.

1 Tbsp Creole seasoning (see Notes)
3 cloves garlic, minced
1/4 tsp kosher salt
Juice of 1 lime
2 Tbsp olive oil
30 medium shrimp, peeled and
    deveined (see Notes)

1. Preheat broiler, with rack set 3–4 inches from heat element.
2. In a large bowl, whisk together Creole seasoning, garlic, salt, lime juice, and olive oil.
3. Add shrimp to mixture, and toss gently until well coated.
4. Spread shrimp in a single layer on baking sheet.
5. Broil shrimp 2–3 minutes. Using tongs, turn each shrimp over and broil 2–3 minutes more, until pink and opaque.

Serves: 6
Serving Size: 5 shrimp
Prep Time: 10 minutes
Cook Time: 6 minutes

Choices/Exchanges

1 Lean Protein, 1/2 Fat

Basic Nutritional Values

Calories	80
Calories from Fat	40
Total Fat	4.5 g
Saturated Fat	0.6 g
Trans Fat	0.0 g
Cholesterol	65 mg
Sodium	120 mg
Potassium	115 mg
Total Carbohydrate	2 g
Dietary Fiber	0 g
Sugars	0 g
Protein	9 g
Phosphorus	90 mg

Notes:
- I am into quick and easy. That is why I like to use Creole seasoning, which is typically a blend of equal parts cayenne pepper, garlic powder, black pepper, salt, and paprika.
- It is best to use fresh (never frozen) shrimp. If that is not possible, use shrimp that are free of preservatives (for example, shrimp that have not been treated with salt or STPP [sodium tripolyphosphate]).

Savory Sides

Side dishes are a bridge-full of flavor in Tex-Mex cooking. Tangy slaws, simple beans, and fresh greens laced with spicy honey and citrus make you crave more. They add life to any meal. I have focused on reducing fat, lowering carbohydrates, and reducing calories. Here is an offering of healthy dishes you will make again and again.

Mexican Rice 160

Green Chile Rice 161

Zucchini and Corn Medley (Calabacitas) 162

Tangy Mexican Slaw 163

Pinto Beans 164

Refried Beans 165

Fresh-Mex Greens with Chipotle Honey Sauce 166

Papas and Queso 167

Chopped Mexican Salad with Lime 169

Mexican Rice

Serves: 8
Serving Size: 1/2 cup
Prep Time: 15 minutes
Cook Time: 32 minutes

Choices/Exchanges

1 1/2 Starch, 1/2 Fat

Basic Nutritional Values

Calories	150
Calories from Fat	40
Total Fat	4.5 g
Saturated Fat	0.7 g
Trans Fat	0.0 g
Cholesterol	0 mg
Sodium	220 mg
Potassium	200 mg
Total Carbohydrate	26 g
Dietary Fiber	2 g
Sugars	2 g
Protein	3 g
Phosphorus	110 mg

This traditional side dish is full of flavor. Fresh garlic, minced onion, and tomato season this rice with Spanish-style flavors.

2 Tbsp light olive oil
1/2 cup minced onion
3 cloves garlic, minced
1 1/4 cups long-grain brown rice
1 cup no-salt-added tomato sauce
3 cups water
3/4 tsp salt
2 1/2 oz fresh asparagus, cooked and finely chopped

1. In a large skillet, heat oil over medium heat. Sauté onion and garlic until onion is transparent, 4–6 minutes. Add rice and sauté until rice starts to brown lightly, 4–6 minutes.
2. Slowly add tomato sauce, water, and salt and blend well. Bring to a boil.
3. Reduce heat to medium-low. Cover and simmer until rice is tender and liquid has evaporated, 15–20 minutes. Fluff rice with a fork, then gently fold in asparagus until well blended.

Variation: Omit the salt and add a salt-free seasoning blend (such as Mrs. Dash) instead.

Tips

- If rice does not have a soft texture after cooking as directed, reduce heat to low and cook, covered, for another 5–10 minutes, being careful not to burn the rice on the bottom of pan.
- If rice does have a soft texture after cooking as directed, but some liquid remains in pan, continue cooking rice, uncovered, until liquid has evaporated.

Green Chile Rice

This rice dish, accented with fresh green chiles and laced with cheese, makes a creamy side.

1 Tbsp olive oil
1/2 cup Roasted Green Chiles (page 152)
2 cloves garlic, minced
2 cups cooked brown or white rice
1/2 oz fresh asparagus, cooked and chopped
1 cup (about 4 oz) shredded reduced-fat Monterey Jack cheese

1. In a large skillet, heat oil over medium-low heat. Sauté chiles and garlic until soft.
2. Add cooked rice and asparagus to the chile mixture, and mix well. Blend in cheese, stirring until melted. Serve immediately.

Serves: 6
Serving Size: 1/2 cup
Prep Time: 10 minutes
Cook Time: 8 minutes

Choices/Exchanges
1 Starch, 1 Fat

Basic Nutritional Values

Calories	130
Calories from Fat	40
Total Fat	4.5 g
Saturated Fat	1.4 g
Trans Fat	0.0 g
Cholesterol	5 mg
Sodium	65 mg
Potassium	160 mg
Total Carbohydrate	18 g
Dietary Fiber	2 g
Sugars	1 g
Protein	4 g
Phosphorus	115 mg

Zucchini and Corn Medley (Calabacitas)

Serves: 6
Serving Size: 1/2 cup
Prep Time: 20 minutes
Cook Time: 23 minutes

Choices/Exchanges

1/2 Starch, 1 Nonstarchy
Vegetable, 1 1/2 Fat

Basic Nutritional Values

Calories	140
Calories from Fat	50
Total Fat	6.0 g
Saturated Fat	2.5 g
Trans Fat	0.0 g
Cholesterol	15 mg
Sodium	160 mg
Potassium	400 mg
Total Carbohydrate	15 g
Dietary Fiber	3 g
Sugars	4 g
Protein	7 g
Phosphorus	165 mg

This traditional Mexican corn and squash dish is full of texture and creamy goodness.

1 Tbsp olive oil
1/2 cup chopped onion
2 cloves garlic, minced
1/2 cup Roasted Green Chiles (page 152)
1 cup chopped summer squash
2 cups chopped zucchini
2 cups cooked corn
1/2 cup (about 2 oz) shredded reduced-fat Monterey Jack cheese
1/2 cup (about 2 oz) shredded part-skim mozzarella cheese
2 Tbsp reduced-sodium chicken stock
1/2 tsp ground black pepper

1. In a large skillet, heat oil over medium-high heat. Sauté onion, garlic, and chiles until soft, about 3 minutes. Add squash and zucchini and cook until vegetables are tender, about 10–12 minutes.
2. Reduce heat to low and stir in corn, cheeses, stock, and black pepper until cheese is melted and mixture is heated through, 6–8 minutes. Serve immediately.

Tangy Mexican Slaw

A tangy coleslaw makes a great accent for any Mexican meal. Serve this slaw as a side dish or as a garnish for tacos, tortas, or enchiladas.

- 1/3 cup canola oil
- 1/3 cup white vinegar
- 1/2 tsp salt
- 1/2 tsp black pepper
- 3 cups finely shredded green cabbage
- 2 cups finely shredded red cabbage
- 3 green onions, mostly green part, minced
- 1 cup chopped spinach leaves

1. In a large bowl, whisk together oil, vinegar, salt, and pepper until well blended. Add green cabbage, red cabbage, green onions, and spinach and toss until well coated.
2. Refrigerate in an airtight container, stirring occasionally, for up to 1 hour before serving. When covered and refrigerated, this coleslaw will keep for up to 2 days.

Variation: For additional flavor, add juice of 1 lime.

Serves: 6
Serving Size: 1 cup
Prep Time: 15 minutes
Chill Time: 1 hour

Choices/Exchanges

1 Nonstarchy Vegetable,
2 1/2 Fat

Basic Nutritional Values

Calories	130
Calories from Fat	110
Total Fat	12.0 g
Saturated Fat	0.9 g
Trans Fat	0.0 g
Cholesterol	0 mg
Sodium	210 mg
Potassium	170 mg
Total Carbohydrate	5 g
Dietary Fiber	2 g
Sugars	2 g
Protein	1 g
Phosphorus	20 mg

Pinto Beans

Serves: 12
Serving Size: 1/2 cup
Prep Time: 10 minutes
Cook Time: 3 hours

Choices/Exchanges

2 Starch, 1 Lean Protein

Basic Nutritional Values

Calories	170
Calories from Fat	5
Total Fat	0.5 g
Saturated Fat	0.1 g
Trans Fat	0.0 g
Cholesterol	0 mg
Sodium	5 mg
Potassium	690 mg
Total Carbohydrate	31 g
Dietary Fiber	8 g
Sugars	1 g
Protein	11 g
Phosphorus	205 mg

Pinto beans are used in many Tex-Mex dishes. Here is a basic go-to recipe for them, full of fiber and flavor. I often cook up a pot and freeze the beans for convenience later.

3 cups dried pinto beans
1 Tbsp garlic powder
1 Tbsp onion powder

1. Place beans in a large pot. Add enough water to cover by 4 inches, and bring to a boil over medium-high heat.
2. Reduce heat to medium-low, add garlic and onion powders, and boil gently until soft, 2 1/2–3 hours.
3. Turn off heat and let beans cool to room temperature, about 2–3 hours.

Variation: Substitute kidney beans or black beans for the pinto beans. Follow Step 1.

Tips

- Test for doneness by smashing one bean between your thumb and index finger.
- Store beans in an airtight container, and refrigerate for up to 2 days or freeze for up to 4 months.
- Save some of the liquid drained from the cooked beans, and freeze it to be used in other recipes, such as Refried Beans (page 165).

Refried Beans

These beans can be whipped up in minutes. A true, authentic Mexican flavor is best achieved by refrying these beans in lard (used in moderation!). However, canola oil is a fine substitute. The beans are delicious either way.

2 cups Pinto Beans (page 164), drained, reserving liquid
1 1/2 Tbsp lard (see Variation)
1/3 tsp salt

1. In a large skillet, heat cooked beans and 1/4 cup reserved liquid over medium-high heat. Bring to a boil and cook for 2 minutes.
2. Reduce heat to medium-low. Using a potato masher, gently mash beans. Beans should be like a thick paste, not runny. If too thick, add more reserved liquid, 1 tsp at a time, until bean mixture is thick, but not stiff. Repeat until all beans are mashed.
3. In another large skillet, melt lard over medium-high heat. Add mashed beans and salt, and stir until well blended and bubbling, 4–6 minutes.

Variation: Substitute 2 Tbsp vegetable or canola oil for the lard.

Serves: 4
Serving Size: 1/2 cup
Prep Time: 8 minutes
Cook Time: 12 minutes

Choices/Exchanges

2 Starch, 1 Lean Protein, 1/2 Fat

Basic Nutritional Values

Calories	220
Calories from Fat	45
Total Fat	5.0 g
Saturated Fat	2.0 g
Trans Fat	0.0 g
Cholesterol	5 mg
Sodium	200 mg
Potassium	690 mg
Total Carbohydrate	31 g
Dietary Fiber	8 g
Sugars	1 g
Protein	11 g
Phosphorus	205 mg

Fresh-Mex Greens with Chipotle Honey Sauce

Serves: 8
Serving Size: 1 cup salad plus
    1 1/2 Tbsp dressing
Prep Time: 20 minutes
Chill Time: 1 hour

Choices/Exchanges

1/2 Carbohydrate,
1 Nonstarchy Vegetable,
2 Fat

Basic Nutritional Values

Calories	140
Calories from Fat	90
Total Fat	10.0 g
Saturated Fat	1.9 g
Trans Fat	0.0 g
Cholesterol	10 mg
Sodium	180 mg
Potassium	180 mg
Total Carbohydrate	10 g
Dietary Fiber	2 g
Sugars	4 g
Protein	2 g
Phosphorus	65 mg

This nutritious salad is full of a variety of leafy lettuces. The jicama adds texture, while the spicy brown mustard and chipotle chile powder lace this salad with flavor.

Salad

4 cups fresh leafy greens
2 cups fresh baby spinach
1 cup thin strips peeled jicama
1 medium red onion, thinly sliced
1 cup Baked Crispy Corn Tortilla Chips (page 20),
    broken into bite-size pieces
1/4 cup crumbled cotija or feta cheese

Dressing

1/3 cup minced onion
5 Tbsp olive oil
3 Tbsp water
3 Tbsp apple cider vinegar
1/2 tsp zero-calorie granulated sweetener (such as Splenda)
1 Tbsp honey
1/8 tsp salt
1 tsp chipotle chile powder
2 Tbsp spicy brown mustard

1. In a large bowl, gently toss together greens, spinach, jicama, and onion. Cover and refrigerate until chilled, for at least 30 minutes or for up to 4 hours.
2. To make dressing, in a food processor or a blender add onion, oil, water, vinegar, zero-calorie granulated sweetener, honey, salt, chipotle powder, and mustard. Process until smooth. Refrigerate in an airtight container for 1 hour or for up to 2 weeks.
3. When ready to serve, pour dressing over greens mixture and toss to coat. Top with tortilla chips and cheese. Serve immediately.

Papas and Queso

This hearty dish can be served for breakfast, lunch, or dinner. The rich queso complements the crispy texture of the potatoes.

4 medium baking potatoes (scrubbed, unpeeled), cut into 1-inch pieces
2 Tbsp vegetable oil
1/4 tsp seasoned salt
3/4 cup Classic Queso Sauce (page 54), warmed
3 green onions, mostly green part, minced
1 Tbsp cilantro

1. Cook potatoes in the microwave on high for 2 minutes. Turn and cook 2 minutes more. Transfer to cutting board, cool slightly, and cut into bite-size pieces.
2. In a skillet, heat oil over medium-high heat. Add potatoes and season with salt. Cook, stirring occasionally, until golden brown and crispy, 8–10 minutes.
3. Place potatoes on a serving platter and top with Classic Queso Sauce, green onions, and cilantro.

Serves: 8
Serving Size: 3/4 cup
Prep Time: 10 minutes
Cook Time: 12 minutes

Choices/Exchanges
1 Starch, 1 1/2 Fat

Basic Nutritional Values

Calories	150
Calories from Fat	60
Total Fat	7.0 g
Saturated Fat	2.3 g
Trans Fat	0.0 g
Cholesterol	10 mg
Sodium	230 mg
Potassium	330 mg
Total Carbohydrate	16 g
Dietary Fiber	1 g
Sugars	2 g
Protein	6 g
Phosphorus	210 mg

Chopped Mexican Salad with Lime

This fresh chopped salad is full of color. A citrus marinade drizzled over the veggies brings them to life. I serve this salad as a lovely side dish or as an entrée.

Dressing
- 1/2 cup fresh-squeezed lime juice
- 1/4 cup olive oil
- 1 tsp crushed red pepper flakes
- 3 cloves garlic, minced
- 1 1/2 Tbsp honey

Salad
- 6 cups chopped romaine lettuce
- 1 (15-oz) can black beans, rinsed and drained
- 1 cup peeled, chopped jicama
- 1 (15-oz) can corn, drained
- 1 red bell pepper, seeded, cored and diced
- 2 ripe avocados, peeled and diced
- 1/2 cup (about 2 oz) shredded reduced-fat Monterey Jack cheese

1. To make the dressing, in a small bowl whisk together lime juice, olive oil, crushed red pepper flakes, garlic, and honey. Dressing is best served at room temperature.
2. Spread lettuce evenly across a large serving platter. Arrange beans, jicama, corn, bell pepper, and avocados side by side on top of lettuce. Garnish with cheese. Cover and refrigerate until chilled, for at least 1 hour. Drizzle with dressing before serving.

Serves: 8
Serving Size: 1 1/2 cups
Prep Time: 15 minutes
Chill Time: 1 hour

Choices/Exchanges

1 Starch, 1/2 Carbohydrate,
1 Nonstarchy Vegetable,
3 Fat

Basic Nutritional Values

Calories	240
Calories from Fat	140
Total Fat	15.0 g
Saturated Fat	2.8 g
Trans Fat	0.0 g
Cholesterol	5 mg
Sodium	180 mg
Potassium	510 mg
Total Carbohydrate	24 g
Dietary Fiber	8 g
Sugars	7 g
Protein	7 g
Phosphorus	130 mg

Little Sweets

The sweetest endings for any Tex-Mex meal start with love. It takes just a little extra time and effort to create a sweet, low-sugar bite, slice, scoop, or square of dessert. Enjoy caramel, sweet creams, fresh and tangy parfaits studded with berries, and rich cakes—all low in sugar and carbs.

Baked Sopapilla Bites 172

Quick Churros with Coconut Sauce 173

Mini Flan Cheesecakes 174

Sweet Tortilla Triangles 175

Tres Leches Parfait 177

Mini Apple Chimichangas 179

Colada Parfait 180

Crispy Ice Cream Scoops with Cajeta Sauce 181

Wine Margarita Sorbet 182

Mi Chocolate Cake 183

Saucy Pralines 184

Baked Sopapilla Bites

Serves: 12

Serving Size: 2 bites plus 1/2 cup raspberries

Prep Time: 12 minutes

Cook Time: 15 minutes

Choices/Exchanges

1/2 Starch, 1/2 Fruit, 1/2 Carbohydrate, 1 Fat

Basic Nutritional Values

Calories	150
Calories from Fat	45
Total Fat	5.0 g
Saturated Fat	2.5 g
Trans Fat	0.0 g
Cholesterol	0 mg
Sodium	70 mg
Potassium	190 mg
Total Carbohydrate	26 g
Dietary Fiber	5 g
Sugars	14 g
Protein	2 g
Phosphorus	30 mg

Puff pastry allows the authentic flavor of this little Mexican pastry to be recreated in a healthy way. The recipe combines sugar, cinnamon, and a drizzle of honey on crisp and flaky puff pastry squares—simply delicious!

6 Tbsp zero-calorie granulated sweetener (such as Splenda)
1 Tbsp ground cinnamon
1 sheet puff pastry (see Note), thawed
3 Tbsp honey
6 cups fresh raspberries

1. Preheat oven to 400°F.
2. In a large bowl, combine zero-calorie granulated sweetener and cinnamon. Set aside.
3. Unfold pastry sheet on a lightly floured surface.
4. Cut the pastry sheet into 24 (2-inch) squares. Place pastry squares on a baking sheet and bake for 12–15 minutes, until the pastries are golden brown.
5. Carefully toss hot pastries, a few at a time, in the sugar mixture.
6. For each serving, place two bites on a plate, drizzle lightly with honey, and garnish with 1/2 cup raspberries.

Note: One sheet is one-half of a 17.3-oz package of puff pastry sheets.

Quick Churros with Coconut Sauce

I love churros, but the crispy, sweet doughnut-like treats can be full of calories. This recipe offers the same taste in a different way: angel food cake, sweetened and lightly baked. Delicious!

6 Tbsp zero-calorie granulated sweetener (such as Splenda)
1 tsp ground cinnamon
1 medium-sized store-bought angel food cake, cut into 24 (1-inch) cubes
Cooking spray
3 Tbsp cream of coconut
5 Tbsp almond milk
1/8 tsp salt
4 cups fresh raspberries

1. Preheat oven to 400°F.
2. In a medium-sized bowl, combine zero-calorie granulated sweetener and cinnamon. Set aside.
3. Place cake cubes on wax paper. Spray each cube lightly with cooking spray, turning each cube over to get all sides. Quickly toss cake cubes by small batches in the granulated sweetener mixture, then place on a baking sheet.
4. Bake for 7 minutes, until lightly browned. Turn each cube over and bake for 5 minutes on the other side until golden brown and crispy. Remove from oven and cool to room temperature.
5. In a small saucepan, combine cream of coconut, almond milk, and salt over low heat. Stir until well blended and warmed through. Transfer sauce to a small bowl, and serve on a platter with cake bites and raspberries.

Serves: 8
Serving Size: 3 churros, 1 Tbsp coconut sauce, and 1/2 cup raspberries
Prep Time: 15 minutes
Cook Time: 12 minutes

Choices/Exchanges
1/2 Fruit, 1/2 Carbohydrate, 1/2 Fat

Basic Nutritional Values

Calories	90
Calories from Fat	20
Total Fat	2.0 g
Saturated Fat	1.1 g
Trans Fat	0.0 g
Cholesterol	0 mg
Sodium	100 mg
Potassium	120 mg
Total Carbohydrate	19 g
Dietary Fiber	4 g
Sugars	11 g
Protein	2 g
Phosphorus	45 mg

Mini Flan Cheesecakes

Serves: 12

Serving Size: 1 mini cheesecake plus 1/3 cup blueberries and sauce

Prep Time: 20 minutes

Cook Time: 13 minutes

Choices/Exchanges

1/2 Fruit, 1/2 Carbohydrate, 1 Fat

Basic Nutritional Values

Calories	120
Calories from Fat	45
Total Fat	5.0 g
Saturated Fat	2.6 g
Trans Fat	0.0 g
Cholesterol	30 mg
Sodium	160 mg
Potassium	90 mg
Total Carbohydrate	16 g
Dietary Fiber	1 g
Sugars	10 g
Protein	3 g
Phosphorus	45 mg

After a spicy Tex-Mex meal, just a little bit of sweetness is all you need. These miniature cheesecakes are full of flavor, crowned with a caramelized sauce.

12 mini muffin baking cups
12 reduced-fat vanilla wafers, crushed
8 oz reduced-fat cream cheese
1/3 cup zero-calorie granulated sweetener (such as Splenda)
1/2 tsp vanilla extract
1 egg, beaten
1 egg white, beaten
1/4 cup low-calorie brown sugar blend (such as Splenda)
3 Tbsp almond milk
1/4 tsp salt
4 cups fresh blueberries

1. Place mini muffin baking cups in a 12-muffin mini muffin pan.
2. Process vanilla wafers in a food processor, then divide evenly into baking cups; press crumbs firmly into cups.
3. In a medium-sized bowl, combine cream cheese, zero-calorie granulated sweetener, vanilla, egg, and egg white. Spoon into each muffin cup.
4. Bake for 10–12 minutes, until raised and slightly browned. Cool to room temperature.
5. In a small saucepan, combine low-calorie brown sugar blend, almond milk, and salt together over medium-low heat until mixture bubbles and is well blended, about 1 minute. Remove from heat.
6. Drizzle sauce over mini cheesecakes, top each serving with 1/3 cup blueberries, and serve.

Sweet Tortilla Triangles

These sweet chips can scoop up delicious citrus salsa or garnish a bowl of sorbet. Baking reduces the fat and calories for a healthy treat.

6 Tbsp zero-calorie granulated sweetener (such as Splenda)
1 tsp cinnamon
4 (8-inch) Fresh Whole-Grain Flour Tortillas (page 70), each cut into
    6 wedges
Cooking spray

1. Preheat oven to 400°F.
2. Combine zero-calorie granulated sweetener and cinnamon in a small mixing bowl.
3. Place the tortilla wedges in a single layer on a cutting board. Spray with cooking spray and sprinkle with half the granulated sweetener and cinnamon mixture.
4. Place wedges on baking sheet, sweetener mixture side down. Spray the top side of each wedge, and sprinkle with remaining granulated sweetener mixture. Discard any remaining sweetener mixture.
5. Bake tortilla wedges for 7 minutes. Turn each wedge over, and bake for 5 more minutes. Remove from baking sheet, and cool to room temperature.

Serves: 6
Serving Size: 4 chips
Prep Time: 10 minutes
Cook Time: 12 minutes

Choices/Exchanges
1 Starch, 1/2 Fat

Basic Nutritional Values

Calories	110
Calories from Fat	30
Total Fat	3.5 g
Saturated Fat	0.3 g
Trans Fat	0.0 g
Cholesterol	0 mg
Sodium	160 mg
Potassium	65 mg
Total Carbohydrate	17 g
Dietary Fiber	2 g
Sugars	1 g
Protein	3 g
Phosphorus	55 mg

Tres Leches Parfait

Tres Leches means "three milks." This combination makes a sweet sauce that's perfect for drenching a fruity parfait.

1/4 cup reduced-calorie sweetened condensed milk
1/4 cup evaporated skim milk
1/2 cup unsweetened vanilla almond milk
2 cups strawberries, chopped
2 cups blueberries
1 medium-sized store-bought angel food cake or loaf, cut into 32 (1-inch) cubes
4 Tbsp sweetened whipped cream
Zest of 1 small lemon

1. In a medium-sized bowl, combine sweetened condensed milk, evaporated milk, and almond milk. Mix well.
2. Combine strawberries and blueberries in another bowl.
3. Place 2 cake cubes in each parfait glass. Top with 1/2 cup of berries. Place 2 cake cubes on top of berries.
4. Top each with 2 Tbsp sauce and 1/2 Tbsp of whipped cream.
5. Garnish with lemon zest.

Serves: 8
Serving Size: 1 parfait
Prep Time: 20 minutes
Cook Time: N/A

Choices/Exchanges

1/2 Fruit, 1 Carbohydrate, 1/2 Fat

Basic Nutritional Values

Calories	120
Calories from Fat	20
Total Fat	2.0 g
Saturated Fat	1.1 g
Trans Fat	0.0 g
Cholesterol	5 mg
Sodium	110 mg
Potassium	190 mg
Total Carbohydrate	24 g
Dietary Fiber	2 g
Sugars	17 g
Protein	3 g
Phosphorus	95 mg

Mini Apple Chimichangas

This hand-held apple fritter is easy to make. Whole-wheat tortillas are filled with a sweet apple filling and baked to perfection.

2 apples, cored and chopped
3 Tbsp zero-calorie granulated sweetener (such as Splenda), divided use
1/2 tsp cinnamon
1/4 cup water
4 (8-inch) Fresh Whole-Grain Flour Tortillas (page 70)
Cooking spray

1. Preheat oven to 400°F.
2. In a medium-sized saucepan, combine apples, 2 Tbsp zero-calorie granulated sweetener, cinnamon, and water. Bring to a boil, and cook until apples are soft. Remove from heat. Cool to room temperature.
3. To build the chimichangas, pile 2 tsp apple filling on each tortilla and fold each end over the filling. Roll the tortillas up and secure each one with a toothpick. Lightly coat the tortillas with cooking spray. Place folded tortillas seam side down on baking sheet. Sprinkle evenly with remaining granulated sweetener. Bake for 5 minutes, then turn over and bake for 5 minutes more.
4. Remove chimichangas from baking sheet and place on individual plates. If desired, garnish each with a scoop of ice cream or a dollop of whipped cream.

Serves: 4
Serving Size: 1 chimichanga
Prep Time: 15 minutes
Cook Time: About 15 minutes

Choices/Exchanges
1 1/2 Starch, 1/2 Fruit, 1 Fat

Basic Nutritional Values

Calories.................200
Calories from Fat 50
Total Fat ....6.0 g
Saturated Fat ....0.6 g
Trans Fat ....0.0 g
Cholesterol .... 0 mg
Sodium .... 240 mg
Potassium .... 170 mg
Total Carbohydrate....... 33 g
Dietary Fiber .... 5 g
Sugars................. 8 g
Protein .... 4 g
Phosphorus........... 90 mg

Colada Parfait

Serves: 8
Serving Size: 1 parfait
Prep Time: 15 minutes
Cook Time: About 4 minutes

Choices/Exchanges

1/2 Fruit,
1 1/2 Carbohydrate

Basic Nutritional Values

Calories	130
Calories from Fat	20
Total Fat	2.0 g
Saturated Fat	1.4 g
Trans Fat	0.0 g
Cholesterol	0 mg
Sodium	125 mg
Potassium	95 mg
Total Carbohydrate	28 g
Dietary Fiber	2 g
Sugars	20 g
Protein	2 g
Phosphorus	45 mg

This is a simple and refreshing dessert full of beautiful fruit and a festive flavor. Start with angel food cake, add berries, and top it with a light colada sauce.

1/4 cup cream of coconut
1/2 cup pineapple juice
1/4 cup almond milk
1/8 tsp salt
1 medium-sized store-bought angel food cake, cut into 32 (1-inch) cubes
1 cup fat-free pineapple sorbet
1 cup fresh blueberries
1 cup fresh raspberries

1. In a small saucepan over medium-low heat, combine cream of coconut, pineapple juice, almond milk, and salt. Stir until well blended and heated through. Remove and cool.
2. Divide half of the cubed cake evenly among 8 Collins glasses. Divide sorbet evenly among glasses. Divide blueberries evenly among glasses.
3. Top glasses evenly with remaining cake.
4. Drizzle each parfait with coconut sauce, and top evenly with raspberries.

Crispy Ice Cream Scoops with Cajeta Sauce

This "deep-fried" ice cream is not deep-fried at all! Just a crispy sweet coating wrapped around a creamy scoop of ice cream. Add the caramel—*cajeta* (pronounced *kah-heh-tah*)—sauce, and the result is blissfully good.

1 quart frozen vanilla reduced-fat yogurt
2 cups corn flakes, crushed
1/4 cup minced pecans
2 Tbsp zero-calorie granulated sweetener (such as Splenda)
1 tsp cinnamon
2 Tbsp low-calorie brown sugar blend (such as Splenda)
2 Tbsp almond milk
3 cups raspberries

1. Line a freezer-proof pie plate or loaf pan with wax paper. Scoop yogurt into 12 individual 1/3-cup servings (use a #12 scoop), about 2 1/2 inches round, and place the scoops on the pie plate. Cover with wax paper and freeze until firm, 3–6 hours.
2. Combine corn flakes, pecans, zero-calorie granulated sweetener, and cinnamon in a medium-sized bowl. Mix well. Remove 2 Tbsp of corn flake mixture and set aside.
3. Remove frozen yogurt scoops from the freezer. Immediately roll each scoop individually in the corn flake mixture, coating well. Place scoops back on the freezer-proof plate and return to the freezer for 1 hour.
4. In a small saucepan, combine low-calorie brown sugar blend and almond milk over medium-low heat. Blend well and cook until brown sugar blend is completely dissolved and sauce is thickened.
5. Just before serving, place a scoop frozen yogurt in each serving bowl and drizzle with the warm sauce.
6. Garnish each serving with 1/4 cup raspberries, and sprinkle remaining cornflake mixture evenly among the bowls.

Serves: 12
Serving Size: 1/3 cup frozen yogurt, sauce, and 1/4 cup raspberries
Prep Time: 25 minutes
Chill Time: 4 hours
Cook Time: 4 minutes

Choices/Exchanges
1 1/2 Carbohydrate, 1/2 Fat

Basic Nutritional Values

Calories	130
Calories from Fat	30
Total Fat	3.5 g
Saturated Fat	1.1 g
Trans Fat	0.0 g
Cholesterol	10 mg
Sodium	75 mg
Potassium	115 mg
Total Carbohydrate	24 g
Dietary Fiber	2 g
Sugars	13 g
Protein	2 g
Phosphorus	45 mg

Wine Margarita Sorbet

Serves: 6

Serving Size: 1/2 cup

Prep Time: 15 minutes

Chill Time: 3 hours

Choices/Exchanges

1/2 Carbohydrate,
1/2 Alcohol

Basic Nutritional Values

Calories	90
Calories from Fat	0
Total Fat	0.0 g
Saturated Fat	0.0 g
Trans Fat	0.0 g
Cholesterol	0 mg
Sodium	60 mg
Potassium	130 mg
Total Carbohydrate	9 g
Dietary Fiber	1 g
Sugars	5 g
Protein	3 g
Phosphorus	85 mg

This dessert is a luscious blend of sorbet and wine. So refreshing! The perfect finish to a Tex-Mex dinner.

Countertop ice cream maker, ready to use
1 cup boiling water
1 (0.30-oz) package sugar-free lime-flavored gelatin
2 1/2 cups light beer, divided use
1 (1.8-g) packet powdered sugar-free lemonade concentrate (such as Crystal Light)
1 (5.3-oz) container key lime–flavored Greek yogurt (such as Dannon Light & Fit 80 Calories)
6 oz sparkling white wine
3 mandarin oranges (Halo brand or Cuties brand), peeled and sectioned

1. In a medium-sized bowl, combine boiling water and gelatin until dissolved completely. Add 1 cup light beer, stirring as it foams up, and mix well. Set aside.
2. In a separate bowl, combine sugar-free lemonade mix with yogurt and 1 1/2 cups light beer.
3. Turn on the ice cream maker, and gently pour both mixtures in at the same time. Use ice cream maker as directed, churning mixture until firm, about 30–45 minutes.
4. Place mixture in a freezer-proof container, and freeze for 3 hours or up to a week.
5. To serve, divide sorbet into individual stemmed glasses. Drizzle 1 Tbsp of wine over each serving, garnish with orange pieces, and serve immediately.

Mi Chocolate Cake

I love this little treat. A cake all to myself! Its rich chocolate flavor and smooth texture make this single-serving dessert a keeper.

1 tsp canola oil
2 Tbsp almond milk
1 egg
1/4 tsp vanilla extract
2 Tbsp zero-calorie granulated sweetener (such as Splenda)
2 Tbsp cocoa powder
2 Tbsp whole-wheat flour
1/4 tsp baking powder
1/2 cup strawberries, stemmed, rinsed, and chopped
1/8 tsp cinnamon

1. In a small bowl, combine oil, almond milk, egg, and vanilla. Blend well.
2. In another small bowl, combine zero-calorie granulated sweetener, cocoa powder, flour, and baking powder. Mix well.
3. Slowly pour egg mixture into flour mixture and blend well.
4. Pour batter into a 4 1/2-oz ramekin, and microwave on high for 1 minute. Remove and cool for 8–10 minutes.
5. Invert cake onto a dessert plate. Garnish with strawberries and sprinkle with cinnamon. Top with whipped cream if desired (optional).

Serves: 1
Serving Size: 1 cake
Prep Time: 12 minutes
Cook Time: 1 minute

Choices/Exchanges

2 Carbohydrate,
1 Medium-Fat Protein

Basic Nutritional Values

Calories	190
Calories from Fat	60
Total Fat	7.0 g
Saturated Fat	2.5 g
Trans Fat	0.0 g
Cholesterol	185 mg
Sodium	190 mg
Potassium	450 mg
Total Carbohydrate	27 g
Dietary Fiber	7 g
Sugars	7 g
Protein	11 g
Phosphorus	365 mg

Saucy Pralines

Serves: 32
Serving Size: 1/2 Tbsp
Prep Time: 10 minutes
Cook Time: 8 minutes

Choices/Exchanges
1/2 Carbohydrate, 1/2 Fat

Basic Nutritional Values

Calories	60
Calories from Fat	35
Total Fat	4.0 g
Saturated Fat	1.1 g
Trans Fat	0.1 g
Cholesterol	4 mg
Sodium	15 mg
Potassium	25 mg
Total Carbohydrate	5 g
Dietary Fiber	0 g
Sugars	3 g
Protein	0 g
Phosphorus	15 mg

Pralines are known as the ultimate Tex-Mex dessert—or Mexican candy! Moderation is key, as this recipe contains both butter and sugar. Still, just half a tablespoon of this sweetness will absolutely transform a scoop of reduced-fat sugar-free ice cream or yogurt. Or drizzle a little over a slice of angel food cake and enjoy!

1 cup chopped pecans
1/2 cup low-calorie brown sugar blend (such as Splenda)
1/3 cup fat-free half-and-half
1/4 cup butter
1/2 cup powdered sugar
1 tsp vanilla extract

1. Preheat oven to 250°F.
2. Place pecans on a baking sheet or shallow pan and bake for 6–8 minutes or until pecans are toasted and fragrant.
3. In a medium-sized saucepan, bring low-calorie brown sugar blend, half-and-half, and butter to a boil over medium heat, stirring constantly. Boil for about 1 minute. Remove from heat, and whisk in powdered sugar and vanilla until smooth. Stir in toasted pecans.
4. Immediately spoon 1/2 Tbsp sauce over reduced-fat low-sugar ice cream or frozen yogurt, or over a slice of angel food cake.

For later use: Cool sauce to room temperature and refrigerate for up to 1 week. Reheat on stovetop over low heat or in microwave on low until consistency allows sauce to be drizzled, about 2–3 minutes.

Index

Alphabetical Index

Note: Page numbers in **bold** refer to photographs.

A

Agua Frescas, 2

Albondigas, **94**, 95

alcohol, xxi, 3–4, 6–10, 13–15, 182. *See also* cocktail; *under specific type*

almond milk, xx, 17, 36, 87, 173, 177, 180

American Diabetes Association, xv, xxi

angel food cake, 173, 177, 180

appetizer. *See* starters

apple, 179

artichoke heart, xvii, 36

asparagus, 135, 161

avocado, 29–31, 83, 85, 105, 116, 149, 169

Avocado Corn Soft Tacos, 122

B

bacon, 79, 84, 119

Baked Chicken Flautas, 131

Baked Chile Rellenos, 150

Baked Crispy Corn Tortilla Chips, 20

Baked Crispy Corn Tortilla Chips, 26–28, 32, 83, 166

Baked Sopapilla Bites, 172

Baked Tostada Shells, 74

barbecue sauce, 115

bean

  Bean and Cheese Chimichangas, 142

  Bean and Rice Flautas, 132

  black, xx, 121, 169

  Black Bean Layered Spread, 32

  kidney, xx

  nutrient, xx

  pinto, xx

  Pinto Beans, 164

  red, xx

  Refried Beans, 24, 103, 105, 132, 142

  Refried Beans, 165

  Spicy Black Bean Tacos, 121

beef

  broth, 61, 95

  ground, 27, 95

  Red Chile Beefy Street Enchiladas, 147

  Shredded Beef, 37, 110, 139, 149

  Shredded Beef, 153

  sirloin, 99, 112, 153

  skirt steak, 108, 111

beer, 13, 182

berries, xix, 11–12. *See also under specific type*

bites and starters. *See* starters

Black Bean Layered Spread, 32

blood glucose level, xiii–xiv

blood pressure, xiii

blueberry, 86, 89, 174, 177, 180

boysenberry jam, 65

bread

  French, 33

  Light Sopapillas, 73

  Mexican Bread Pudding with Fresh Berries, **88**, 89

  pita, 21

  Sandwich Thins, 149

  Savory Stuffed Sopapillas, 151

  whole wheat, 85, 87, 89

  Whole-Wheat Morning Toast with Cajeta and Coconut, 87

breakfast

  Breakfast Quesadilla, **78**, 79

  Chilaquiles with Eggs, 83

  Chile Papas, 84

  Chorizo, Potato, and Egg Burrito—Smothered, 82

  Huevos Rancheros, 81

  Mexican Bread Pudding with Fresh Berries, **88**, 89

  Pan Huevos with Avocado, 85

  Spiced Fresh Fruit and Yogurt Parfait, 86

  Tex-Mex Breakfast Tacos, 80

  Whole-Wheat Morning Toast with Cajeta and Coconut, 87

burrito

  Bean and Cheese Chimichangas, 142

  Chile Verde Burritos, **140**, 141

  Chorizo, Potato, and Egg Burrito—Smothered, 82

  Fiber-Full Burrito Bowls, 138

  Machaca Burritos, 139

butternut squash, xix

C

cabbage, 58, 115, 126, 129–130, 163

carbohydrate, xi, xvii

cayenne pepper, xvi

Ceviche, 22

Ceviche Tostadas, 105

champagne, 6

Charred Corn and Avocado Toss, 31

cheese

  American, 36

  Bean and Cheese Chimichangas, 142

  cheddar, 26, 32, 35, 54, 79, 93, 103, 146–147, 150

  Cheesy Green Chile Enchiladas, 143

  cotija, 28, 104, 122, 130, 166

  flavor essentials, xix

  jalapeño, 119

  Mexican, xix

  Monterey Jack, 28, 42–44, 80, 97, 123, 147, 150

  parmesan, 120

  processed, 36, 54

Roasted Green Chile Cheese Crisp,
40, 41
*Smoked Cheddar Cheese and Green
Chile Tamales,* 133–134
Tex-Mex Cheese Enchiladas, **144**, 145
white cheddar, 28, 35
cheesecake, 174
Cheesy Green Chile Enchiladas, 143
chicken, 141, 143
Baked Chicken Flautas, 131
*Chicken and Sweet Potato Quesadil-
las,* 44
Chicken Tacos Verde, 117
Chicken Tortilla Soup, 97
Grilled Mesquite Chicken Tacos, 118
Shredded Chicken, 44, 103, 109, 117,
131, 138, 146
Shredded Chicken, 155
Speedy Roasted Chicken Soft Tacos, 116
Chilaquiles with Eggs, 83
chile
Anaheim/New Mexico, xv
Baked Chile Rellenos, 150
Cheesy Green Chile Enchiladas, 143
Chile Bruschetta, 33
Chile con Carne Tostadas, **106**, 107
Chile con Queso, **34**, 35
Chile Cream Sauce, 60
Chile Cream Sauce, 120
Chile Papas, 84
Chile Pinwheels, 38
Chile Verde Burritos, **140**, 141
chipotle chile in adobo sauce, xv,
113, 115
chipotle chile powder, xvii
fresh, xv–xvi
Fresh Green Chile Guacamole, 30
green, 117. *See also* roasted green
Green Chile Corn Chowder, **92**, 93
Green Chile Enchilada Sauce, 64
Green Chile Rice, 161
Green Chile Stew, 98
Pineapple and Chile Quesadillas, 43

poblano, xvi, 120
pods, dried red, xv
powder, xvi, 61
Red Chile Beefy Street Enchiladas, 147
Red Chile Pork, 154
Red Chile Posole, 96
Red Chile Purée, 63
Red Chile Purée, 66
roasted green, 31, 33, 35, 38, 49–50, 60,
79, 84, 139, 141
Roasted Green Chile Cheese Crisp,
40, 41
Roasted Green Chiles, 30, 62, 133–134,
150
Roasted Green Chiles, 152
roasted poblano, 120
serrano, xv, 48
*Smoked Cheddar Cheese and Green
Chile Tamales,* 133–134
Sour Cream Green Chile Enchiladas,
146
yellow, xv
Chipotle BBQ Pork Soft Tacos, 115
chipotle chile in adobo sauce, xv, 113,
115
chipotle chile powder, xvii
chocolate, 17
cholesterol, xiii, xx
Chopped Mexican Salad with Lime,
168, 169
chorizo, 80
*Chorizo, Potato, and Egg Burrito–
Smothered,* 82
cilantro, xvi, 22–23, 96
cinnamon, xvii
Citrusy Salsa, 51
Classic Crispy Tacos, 109
Classic Guacamole, 29
Classic Guacamole, 32, 138
Classic Queso Sauce, 27, 167
Classic Queso Sauce, 54
Classic Rolled Tacos, 110
club soda, 11

cocktail
Agua Frescas, 2
Fresco White Sangria, 11
Fresh Mexican Mimosa, 6
Fresh Tequila Sunrise, 4
Frozen Margarita, 9
Fruity Red Sangria, 12
Margarita Martini, 3
Margarita Rounds, 7
Michelada, 13, **140**
Paloma Fresco, 15
Sparkling Margarita Punch, 8
Spicy Margarita, **5**, 10
*Tequila Shots and Sangrita
Chaser,* 14
cocoa powder, 17, 183
coconut, 87
coconut, cream of, 173, 180
cod, 126
coffee liqueur, 16
Colada Parfait, 180
Coleslaw Relish, 58
corn, xviii, 28, 31, 52, 93, 122, 162, 169
corn flakes, 181
corn husk, 133–135, 137
cream cheese, 38–39, 174
*Crispy Ice Cream Scoops with Cajeta
Sauce,* 181
Crispy Zucchini Tacos, 123
cumin, xvii

D
dairy, xix
dehydration, xiii
dementia, xiv
depression, xiii
dressing, 166, 169

E
egg, 81–83, 150
enchilada, 143–148
ethnic cuisine, xi
evaporated skim milk, 177

F

Fajita Tacos, 108
fat, xx
Fiber-Full Burrito Bowls, 138
fish, xxi, 22, 126–127
flat-leaf parsley, xvi, 59
flavor essentials, xv–xxii
Fresco White Sangria, 11
Fresh Corn Tortillas, 72
Fresh Green Chile Guacamole, 30
Fresh Green Chile Guacamole, 112
*Fresh-Mex Greens with Chipotle Honey
    Sauce*, 166
Fresh Mexican Mimosa, **5**, 6
Fresh Tequila Sunrise, 4, **5**
Fresh Veggie Enchilada Sauce, 62
Fresh Whole-Grain Flour Tortillas,
    37–39, 41–44, 79, 82, 132, 139, 141–142,
    146, 175, 179
*Fresh Whole-Grain Flour Tortillas
    (8-inch)*, 70
*Fresh Whole-Grain Flour Tortillas
    (10-inch)*, 71
Frijoles Tostadas, 103
Frozen Margarita, 9
fruit, xiii, xix, 86. *See also under
    specific type*
Fruity Red Sangria, 12

G

gelatin, 7, 182
grain, xviii
grapefruit, 15
gravy, 61
Green Chile Corn Chowder, **92**, 93
Green Chile Enchilada Sauce, 64
Green Chile Enchilada Sauce, 82, 141,
    143
Green Chile Rice, 161
Green Chile Stew, 98
greens, xvii–xviii, 105, 118, 121, 125, 138,
    148, 166
Grilled Carne Asada Tacos, 111

Grilled Halibut Tacos, 127
Grilled Mesquite Chicken Tacos, 118
guacamole, 29–30

H

half-and-half, 54, 89, 93, 184
halibut, 127
heart disease, xiv
herb, xiii, xvi, 104. *See also under
    specific type*
hot pepper flakes, xvii
Huevos Rancheros, 81
hummus, 25
hydration, xiii

I

ingredient, xviii
Italian parsley, xvi

J

jalapeño, 22, 26, 39, 48, 51, 57, 149
Jalapeño Pinwheels, 39
jicama, 166, 169
Jicama Salsa, 59

K

kitchen tool, xxii
kiwi, 86

L

legume, xx
lemonade concentrate, 182
lemon/lemon juice, 11–12, 59, 111,
    177
lettuce, 103–104, 107, 109, 119, 127, 139–142,
    148–149, 169
lifestyle trend, xiii–xiv
Light Sopapillas, 73
Light Sopapillas, 151
lime/lime juice, 2–4, 8–9, 13–14, 22–23,
    51–52, 55, 112–114, 169
low-fat, xix

M

Machaca Burritos, 139
Margarita Martini, 3
margarita mix, 10
Margarita Rounds, 7
masa harina, 72, 133–135, 137
mesquite seasoning, 118
Mexican-American cuisine, xi
Mexican beer, 13
*Mexican Bread Pudding with Fresh
    Berries*, **88**, 89
Mexican Café, 16
Mexican Hot Chocolate, 17
Mexican oregano, xvii, 96
Mexican Rice, 138
Mexican Rice, 160
Mexican White Sauce, 53, **56**
Mexican White Sauce, 125–127
Michelada, 13, **140**
Mi Chocolate Cake, 183
milk, xix–xx
Mini Apple Chimichangas, **178**,
    179
Mini Chimis, 37
Mini Flan Cheesecakes, 174
Mini Hummus Tostaditos, 25
Mini Shrimp Shooters., 23
mint, 8, 15
monounsaturated fat, xx

N

No-Beef Taquitos, 128
nut, xx, 181, 184
nutrient, xv, xviii
nutritional information,
    xii

O

omega-3 fatty acid, xxi
onion, xviii, xxi, 55. *See also* Pickled
    Onions
orange/orange juice, 4, 6, 9, 11–12, 14, 51,
    86, 182

P

Paloma Fresco, 15
Pan Huevos with Avocado, 85
panko flakes, 126–127
Papas and Queso, 167
parsley, xvi
peach, 11
pecan, 181, 184
pepper. *See also* chile
    cayenne, xvi
    flakes, xvii, 65, 97
    jalapeño, xv, 22, 26–28, 39, 48, 51, 57,
        111, 149
    orange bell, 108
    pickled jalapeño, xv, 26–28, 111
    red, crushed, 49
    red bell, 57, 95, 108
    roasted red, 25
pickled jalapeño, xv, 26–28, 111
Pickled Onions, 55, **56**
Pickled Onions, 121, 127, 131
Pico de Gallo, 42, 85, 108, 111–113, 126,
    138, 149
Pico de Gallo, 48
Pineapple and Chile Quesadillas, 43
pineapple/pineapple juice, 43, 57, 113,
    180
pineapple sorbet, 180
Pinto Beans, 128, 138, 165
Pinto Beans, 164
Pita Chips, 21
*Poblano and Potato Tacos with Chile
    Cream Sauce*, 120
pork, 96, 113–115, 137, 154
Pork Carnitas Tacos, 114
potato, xviii, 82, 84, 167
puff pastry, 172

Q

Quesadillas de Fresco, 42
Quick Churros with Coconut Sauce, 173
Quick Turkey Club Tacos, 119

R

radish, 96, 148
raspberry, 6, 89, 172–173, 180–181
raspberry jam, 4, 65
Red Chile Beefy Street Enchiladas, 147
Red Chile Pork, 137
Red Chile Pork, 154
Red Chile Posole, 96
Red Chile Purée, 63, 99
Red Chile Purée, 66
Red Chile Tamales, **136**, 137
Red Enchilada Sauce, 63
Red Enchilada Sauce, 82, 96, 147–148
Refried Beans, 24, 103, 105, 132, 142
Refried Beans, 165
reheating tortillas, 75
relish, 58
rice, 132, 138, 160–161
rice milk, xx
Roasted Green Chile Cheese Crisp,
    40, 41
Roasted Green Chiles, 30, 62,
    133–134, 150
Roasted Green Chiles, 152
Roasted Pineapple Salsa, **56**, 57
Roasted Sweet Potato Tostadas, 104
Roasted Tomatillo Chile Sauce, 50, **56**
Roasted Tomatillo Chile Sauce, 83, 117
rosemary, xvi

S

sage, xvi
salad, 166, 169
salsa
    Citrusy Salsa, 51
    Jicama Salsa, 59
    Pico de Gallo, 48
    Roasted Pineapple Salsa, **56**, 57
    Spicy Corn Salsa, 52
    Tex-Mex Salsa, 49
sandwich, 149
sauce

Chile Cream Sauce, 60
Classic Queso Sauce, 54
*Crispy Ice Cream Scoops with Cajeta
    Sauce*, 181
*Fresh-Mex Greens with Chipotle
    Honey Sauce*, 166
Fresh Veggie Enchilada Sauce, 62
Green Chile Enchilada Sauce, 64
Mexican White Sauce, 53
Quick Churros with Coconut Sauce,
    173
Red Chile Purée, 66
Red Enchilada Sauce, 63
Roasted Tomatillo Chile Sauce, 50, **56**
Sweet Chile Sauce, 65
Saucy Loaded Nachos, 27
Saucy Pralines, 184
Savory Mini Tostadas, 24
Savory Stuffed Sopapillas, 151
Seared Sirloin Tacos with Guacamole,
    112
Shredded Beef, 37, 110, 139, 149
Shredded Beef, 153
Shredded Chicken, 44, 103, 109, 117, 131,
    138, 146
Shredded Chicken, 155
shrimp, 23, 125, 156
sides
    Chopped Mexican Salad with Lime,
        168, 169
    *Fresh-Mex Greens with Chipotle
        Honey Sauce*, 166
    Green Chile Rice, 161
    Mexican Rice, 160
    Papas and Queso, 167
    Pinto Beans, 164
    Refried Beans, 165
    Tangy Mexican Slaw, 163
    *Zucchini and Corn Medley
        (Calabacitas)*, **144**, 162
*Smoked Cheddar Cheese and Green
    Chile Tamales*, 133–134
soda, 15